HEAVEN AND END TIMES

DEVOTIONAL AND STUDY BOOK

HEAVEN AND END TIMES
DEVOTIONAL AND STUDY BOOK

Deborah L. Gladwell

HEAVEN AND END TIMES
Copyright © 2022 by Deborah Gladwell. All rights reserved.

No part of this publication may be reproduced, stored in a retrieval system, or transmitted in any way by any means, electronic, mechanical, photocopy, recording, or otherwise without the prior permission of the author except as provided by USA copyright law.

Scripture quotations are taken from the Holy Bible, King James Version, Cambridge, 1769. Used by permission. All rights reserved.

Other Bibles sometimes use different wordings than the King James Version. These Bibles can be used, however; their wording may make some of the questions a little harder to answer.

My conclusions might differ from yours.
"Study to shew thyself approved unto God, a workman that needeth not to be ashamed, rightly dividing the word of truth." 2 Timothy 2:15

Interior design by: Deborah L. Gladwell
Cover design by: Deborah L. Gladwell

Published in the **United States of America**

ISBN 9798407735601

- Nonfiction > Religion > Biblical Studies > Prophecy
- Nonfiction > Religion > Biblical Studies > General

In loving memory of

my Mother and Father

Joyce & Willard Thompson Jr

To my wonderful Husband
Kenny Gladwell
Sons: Kevin and Eric Gladwell
Daughter-in-law: Sara Phillips Gladwell
Sisters: Christine Taylor, Cindy Hulver, Linda Shiflett,
and Suzanne Thompson
Thank you for your love and support
Love you all!

Why Does Man find Salvation Confusing?	1
How Many Judgements do we Face?	5
Judgement Seat of God-Christ	7
The Great White Throne Judgement!	11
Will All Christians Go to Heaven?	15
Firstfruits	18
Rewards and Crowns of Heaven?	21
Are There Different Levels of Heaven?	25
Four Heavens?	28
Even Heaven Has Walls! But, Maybe Not For The Reason You Think!	32
Will we know each other in Heaven?	36
What Will Heaven Look Like?	40
God's Throne in Heaven	45
What does Heaven offer Christians?	48
What will we do in Heaven?	51
Our Mansion in Heaven	55
Will there be Time in Heaven?	58
Purgatory?	61
Is Coronavirus the beginning of the End Times?	66
The Red Heifer!	69
Can You Get Saved After the Rapture?	75
Will Christians go through the Tribulation?	79
Four Horses of Revelation and the Breaking of Seven Seals!	83
The Seven Trumpets You Do Not Want to Hear!	88
Antichrists!	93
The Antichrist!	96
The Entrance of the Antichrist!	99
The Seven Years of the Antichrist and the Seven Vials of God's Wrath!	104
The Antichrist and the False Prophet join forces!	108
Mark of the Beast 666	111
Is The Second Coming and the Rapture the Same Thing!	115
What is the Battle of Armageddon?	120
Millennial Reign of Christ?	125
Battle of Gog and Magog and the Final Judgement	130
Alpha and Omega!	134
What is a World Without Hope?	138
What the Bible Says About the Importance of History	141

Why Does Man find Salvation Confusing?

The main reason many people are confused by the plan of Salvation is that in man's mind it is simply too easy to be true. This reasoning is contrary to God's intentions. God made the plan simple so all could understand it but just as the Pharisees added to the law; man has added to God's plan of salvation.

Man does not understand the deep love God has for man. Humans have limits to their love, God does not.

> For God so loved the world, that he gave his only begotten Son, that whosoever believeth in him should not perish, but have everlasting life.
>
> John 3:16

Some teach that you must do works (good deeds) to obtain and keep your salvation. Not true, you are saved by grace! (*Simple way to look at grace God's Riches At Christ's Expense*).

> For by grace are *ye saved through faith*; and that not of yourselves: *it is the gift of God:*[9] *Not of works, lest any man should boast*. For we are his workmanship, created in Christ Jesus unto good works, which God hath before ordained that we should walk in them.
>
> Ephesians 2:8-10

What is faith? Faith is believing in something even though you cannot see it. The wind is a prime example, you hear it, you see leaves swaying, BUT you cannot see the wind. Is the wind real? Yes! Grace is given to those who have faith. Faith is a requirement for Salvation. If you do not believe Jesus is God's Son who died on the cross and rose again in three days, then you are not saved. Again, this seems too simple, but it is the only legit test to measure the validity of your salvation.

Salvation cannot be lost by sin because notice above, it is the gift of God. A gift is given freely to you. It is YOURS! God is not an Indian giver. He did not put any stipulations on this gift, but do not get excited, it does not mean you can do whatever you want because hey you are saved. God will *not* honor your prayers and may even chastise you, but you are still saved. God knew man would sin and tells us what we must do to get back in his good grace:

> If we confess our sins, he is faithful and just to forgive us our sins, and to cleanse us from all unrighteousness.
>
> 1 John 1:9

Please note the preceding verse is not promoting works but sincerely asking for forgiveness. *None of us will ever be righteous enough* to earn our way or keep our way to heaven. The question is now raised, "If I do not have to work to get to heaven, then why should I serve?" If one is truly saved, they will have a natural love for God and people. The Bible is full of scripture telling us to serve God, but here is an important one,

> Jesus said unto him, **Thou shalt love the Lord thy God with all thy heart, and with all thy soul, and with all thy mind.**[38] This is the first and great commandment.[39] And the second is like unto it, **Thou shalt love thy neighbour as thyself.**[40] On these two commandments hang all the law and the prophets.
> Matthew 22:37-40

The Bible also compares man's own righteous as filthy rags.

> But we are all as an unclean thing, and **all our righteousnesses are as filthy rags**; and we all do fade as a leaf; and our iniquities, like the wind, have taken us away.
> Isaiah 64:6

Salvation in the name of Jesus Christ is the only way we are made righteous. His blood covers us and makes us righteous in the sight of God.

> For he hath made **him** (Jesus) to be sin for us, who knew no sin; that we might be made the righteousness of God in him.
> 2 Corinthians 5:21

God will chastise (rebuke) those who do not do his will.

> As many as I love, I rebuke and chasten: be zealous therefore, and repent.
> Revelation 3:19

> I will be his father, and he shall be my son. If he commit iniquity, I will chasten him with the rod of men, and with the stripes of the children of men:
> 2 Samuel 7:14

Some believe that one must wait to get saved until they clean up their life. False, Satan deceived Eve in the Garden of Eden by using the same type of deception. The Bible teaches that no such restriction is placed on man.

> But God commendeth his love toward us, in that, **while we were yet sinners**, Christ died for us.
> Romans 5:8

Some question their Salvation based on Baptism. It does not matter if you were sprinkled or dunked. The purpose of Baptism is to show others that you accepted Jesus Christ as your Savior. It demonstrates that you believe that God is the ONLY true God and that Jesus is his Son, who died on the cross and rose on the third day! If Baptism saved you then the thief on the cross would not have been able to go to heaven.

*"For by grace are **ye saved through faith**;" Ephesians 2:8a.*

And one of the malefactors which were hanged railed on him, saying, If thou be Christ, save thyself and us.[40] But the other answering rebuked him, saying, Dost not thou fear God, seeing thou art in the same condemnation?[41] And we indeed justly; for we receive the due reward of our deeds: but this man hath done nothing amiss.[42] ***And he said unto Jesus, Lord, remember me when thou comest into thy kingdom.**[43] **And Jesus said unto him, Verily I say unto thee, Today shalt thou be with me in paradise**.*

Luke 23:39-43

How does one obtain Salvation? ***ALL*** anyone must do is believe that Jesus is God's son who died for our sins on the cross. That He rose again from the dead; ask God for forgiveness and call upon Jesus to be your Savior. The Bible says then we are saved.

***For whosoever shall call upon the name of the Lord shall be saved**.*

Romans 10:13

1. Why do you think that God intentionally made the plan of salvation simple?

2. John 3:16, Romans 10:9, Romans 10:13, What does the Bible say one must do to get saved? MUST you believe it, or can you just say the words?

3. According to John 3:16 does the plan of salvation limit who may get saved if they call upon God's name?

4. Romans 5:8, Is it necessary to clean up your life before asking for salvation?

5. Ephesians 2:8-10, States you are saved by grace through _____?

6. Grace is something we do not deserve but Jesus paid the price for us, why do you think that Ephesians 2:8-9 states that we must accept this through faith and not of ourselves?

7. How would you define the word Faith?

8. According to Ephesians 2:8 can you lose your salvation? Explain.

9. 1 John 1:9, If a Christian sins after salvation he does not lose his salvation, but he is disconnected from God until he _____?

10. The Bible says if we had to work for our salvation, we would become boastful therefore God gave salvation as a gift that man must request. What do you think this means?

11. John 14:6, Can we receive salvation solely from any of these sources and why do you feel you can or cannot?
    1. Works
    2. Cleaning up your life
    3. Baptism

12. Isaiah 64:6, Are we ever good enough on our own to get saved?

13. 2 Corinthians 5:21, Nothing can make us righteous in God's eyes except _____?

14. Luke 23:39-43, If baptism is a requirement for salvation would the thief on the cross be saved, would the dying man on his deathbed that accepts salvation be saved?

15. Revelation 3:19, 2 Samuel 7:14, When God chastens us does he love us? Explain.

How Many Judgements do we Face?

Some believe that when we die that is the end of us. They believe our bodies just lie in the ground and deteriorate until we are completely gone. They are partially right however, that is not the end of us.

> All go unto one place; all are of the dust, and all turn to dust again.
> Ecclesiastes 3:20

After death, there are two judgements, one for the saved (those who believe Jesus is God's son and accepted him as their savior) and one judgement for the unsaved (those who believe not that Jesus is God's son and refused him as their savior).

So how do we know there are two separate judgments? We do what any scholar would do, we dive into the Bible.

The Bible says every Christian must be judged for the good or bad they have done while living on earth. This is called the Judgement Seat of Christ.

> For we must all appear before the ***judgment seat of Christ***; that every one may receive the things done in his body, according to that he hath done, whether it be good or bad.
> 2 Corinthians 5:10

We must never forget that none of us are perfect, and we have committed wrongs. But the bright side is we do get rewarded for the good we have done in our lives if our motives were pure.

The Great White Throne Judgement is the last and final judgement. It will be for the unbelievers only.

> And I saw a ***great white throne***, and him that sat on it, from whose face the earth and the heaven fled away; and there was found no place for them. [12] And I saw the dead, small and great, stand before God; and the books were opened: and another book was opened, which is the book of life: and the dead were judged out of those things which were written in the books, according to their works. [13] And the sea gave up the dead which were in it; and death and hell delivered up the dead which were in them: and they were judged every man according to their works. [14] And death and hell were cast into the lake of fire. This is the second death. [15] And whosoever was not found written in the book of life was cast into the lake of fire.
> Revelation 20:11-15

We will dig deeper into these Judgements, rewards, punishments, and the lake of fire in upcoming studies. But we have established, there will be two judgements and who will be at each judgement. With that in mind which will you be at?

This is an introduction to the Judgement seats; therefore, the questions are combined with the questions in the next lesson.

Judgement Seat of God-Christ

What exactly is the Judgement Seat of Christ? When a Christian dies our soul will go before Jesus to be judged for what good or bad we have done in our lives.

> For we must all appear before the judgment seat of Christ; that every one may receive the things done in his body, **according to that he hath done, whether it be good or bad**.
> 2 Corinthians 5:10

> We are confident, I say, and willing rather to be ***absent from the body, and to be present with the Lord.*** *⁹* Wherefore we labour, that, whether present or absent, ***we may be accepted of him.*** *¹⁰ **For we must all appear before the judgment seat of Chris**t*; that every one may receive the things done in his body, according to that he hath done, whether it be good or bad.
> 2 Corinthians 5:8-10

We are promised not to be condemned but that we go from death to life.

> Verily, verily, I say unto you, He that heareth my word, and believeth on him that sent me, hath everlasting life, and ***shall not come into condemnation; but is passed from death unto life.***
> John 5:24

> There is therefore now ***no condemnation to them which are in Christ Jesus***, who walk not after the flesh, but after the Spirit.
> Romans 8:1

Above we see that Christians are not condemned, therefore; we will not be part of the second death which is when the unbelievers are cast into the Lake of Fire. We are told by God that Christians (overcomers) will inherit all things and God will be our God. Unbelievers are banished forever from the sight of God.

> He that overcometh shall inherit all things; and I will be his God, and he shall be my son. ⁸ ***But the fearful, and unbelieving, and the abominable, and murderers, and whoremongers, and sorcerers,***

> *and idolaters, and all liars, shall have their part in the lake which burneth with fire and brimstone: which is the second death.*
>
> Revelation 21:7-8

In the following verse, we find Paul addressing the church. He was not addressing unbelievers. He states that as Christians our foundation must be built on Jesus.

> For other foundation can no man lay than that is laid, which is Jesus Christ.
>
> 1 Corinthians 3:11

Paul instructed that we should strive not to sin, but also assured the Christians that if they did, their Salvation would still be intact. Therefore, we know that this judgement is for the Christian because they are considered saved. Note this Judgement says nothing about anyone being sentenced to Hell or the Lake of Fire.

> If any man's work shall be burned, he shall suffer loss: but he himself shall be saved; yet so as by fire.
>
> 1 Corinthians 3:15

We can also deduce that Christians will be the only ones present at the Judgement Seat of Christ because in the following verse, **"The"** means once so, this means we will not be at the Great White Throne Judgement because that would make two judgements.

> And as it is appointed unto ***men once to die***, but after this ***the judgment***:
>
> Hebrews 9:27

The above verse makes Christians aware that immediately after death we will be judged. The unsaved, as you will see later, are judged at the end of the Millennium. There is no second chance for salvation.

I conclude that only Christians will be at the Judgement seat of Christ and that they will not be at the Great White Throne Judgement. I base this analysis on the fact that Christians go immediately into the presence of Jesus when they die. We will not be condemned and are promised not to suffer the second death. No mention of the Lake of Fire is mentioned at the Judgement Seat of Christ but is at the Great White Throne Judgement.

Keep in mind that just because there is no condemnation toward Christians, does not mean we get a free pass. Most of us will be very ashamed when we are judged; therefore, we should try our best to be Christ-like now. The Judgement Seat of Christ also determines the roles we serve in heaven which we will discuss later.

1. 2 Corinthians 5:10, What is this Judgement called?

2. According to 2 Corinthians 5:10, What is judged?

3. 2 Corinthians 5:10, Revelation 20:11, How many Judgements will there be? _____ What are they called?

4. Romans 2:6, Romans 14:12, What will we give of ourselves?

5. Hebrews 9:27, John 5:24, Revelation 21:7-8; After reading these verses who do you think is present at the Judgement seat of Christ? Explain.

6. 2 Corinthians 5:8, John 5:24, When does the Judgement Seat of God/Christ take place?

7. 1 Corinthians 3:15, Revelation 3:5, If a Christian's work is found unworthy will he lose his Salvation and be tossed out? Explain

8. Romans 2:6,10-11, Psalm 96:13, Will the rich receive special treatment? Explain

9. John 6:28-29, What are the works of God?

10. Romans 8:1, Will Christians be at The Great White Throne Judgement? Explain.

The Great White Throne Judgement!

The Great White Throne Judgement is reserved for those who knowingly rejected salvation through Jesus Christ. Those who believe not that God is the only true and living God. Those who follow Satan because they enjoy their earthly lusts. This judgement should be feared.

Some, as we studied earlier, believe they will just die and turn to dust and that is that. Some believe that there is no hell, only heaven and some believe God is a God of love and will not send anyone to Hell. Well, wrong, wrong, and wrong. There is a day of reckoning for everyone, but if you are present for this one it is baaaaaad! Yes, God is a God of love, he gives each person a free will on earth to accept him or reject him. If you chose to reject him, it is YOU who sent yourself to hell. The Bible has many warnings of such a day of reckoning,

> But after thy hardness and impenitent heart treasurest up unto thyself wrath against **the day of wrath and revelation of the righteous judgment of God**; ⁶Who will render to every man according to his deeds:
> Romans 2:5-6

Is there such a thing as the Great White Throne Judgement? The answer is most definitely yes.

> And I saw **a great white throne**, and him that sat on it, from whose face the earth and the heaven fled away; and there was found no place for them.12 And I saw the dead, small and great, stand before God; and the books were opened: and another book was opened, which is the book of life: and **the dead were judged** out of those things which were written in the books, according to their works.
> Revelation 20:11-12

We know that the Great White Throne Judgement is for the unsaved because the Bible tells us that when Christians die we will pass straight from death to life. We are taken immediately to Jesus.

> Verily, verily, I say unto you, He that heareth my word, and believeth on him that sent me, hath everlasting life, and **shall not come into condemnation; but is passed from death unto life.**
> John 5:24

> We are confident, I say, and willing rather to be absent from the body, and to be present with the Lord.
>
> 2 Corinthians 5:8

The unsaved souls immediately go to hell when they die. They are considered dead and await judgement there. Their wealth and status will not help them at this final judgement,

> And I saw the ***dead, small and great***, stand before God; and ***the books were opened: and another book was opened, which is the book of life***: and ***the dead were judged out of those things which were written in the books, according to their works***. [13] And the sea gave up the dead which were in it; and death and hell delivered up the dead which were in them: and they were judged every man according to their works.
>
> Revelation 20:12-13

What are these open books at the Great White Throne Judgement? Some call the first book, "The book of death". It holds the records of every unsaved person's life. They will be judged according to their works of good or evil. This leads one to believe there might be different levels of torment or burning, but even a little for eternity is too much. Thank goodness if you are saved you will not have to find out if there are different levels of the lake of fire.

> For God shall bring every work into judgment, with every secret thing, whether it be good, or whether it be evil.
>
> Ecclesiastes 12:14

But wait a minute, the book of life is there too, Why? Is it possible that some of these souls are saved? If so, why are they not already with Jesus?

The book of life will be there for one purpose. The purpose is to show the unsaved what they turned down. They were given every opportunity to be in that book but chose not to. They will instantly know they were rightly judged and go to the lake of fire knowing the people in the book of life will not be with them.

The Bible tells us that death and hell will be cast into the lake of fire. What does this mean? It simply means that there will no longer be any reason to have a holding place for those who denied Christ because its occupants will be in the lake of fire.

> And death and hell were cast into the lake of fire. This is the second death.
>
> Revelation 20:14

What does the second death mean? Man, never experienced death until after Adam and Eve sinned. From that point on when a person died, the unsaved went to Hades (Hell) to wait for judgement and the saved went to Heaven. The second death will be for the unsaved. It will be God's final judgement (The Great White Throne Judgement). It not only will be filled with eternal pain but the judged will also know they are forever (dead) separated from God in the lake of fire.

When sinners are cast into the lake of fire, they will know that they had every opportunity to avoid this punishment. They will visibly see the book of life. Many will tell God that there must be a mistake because they are a good person. Some will try to barter with God but have nothing that God wants. He is not interested in our wealth or prestige.

> And whosoever was not found written in the book of life was cast into the lake of fire.
>
> Revelation 20:15

> For there is no respect of persons with God.
> Romans 2:11

I beseech you today, if you have not already done so, please search your heart and decide for salvation through Jesus Christ today.

1. What are some beliefs that will happen to us after we die?

2. Hebrews 10:26-30, As a God of love will God reject people from entering Heaven? Explain your answer.

3. Revelation 20:11, What is this Judgement called?

4. Revelation 20:12, Will the people at the Great White Throne Judgement also be Judged for their deeds?

5. John 5:24, 2 Corinthians 5:8, How do we know Christians will not be present at this Judgement?

6. Revelation 20:12-13, There are two books opened, what are they?

7. Why do you think the book of life will be open? Do you think there will be saved people there? Explain.

8. Romans 5:12, What is the first death?

9. Revelation 20:14, Revelation 21:8, What is the second death?

10. Romans 2:11, Can you buy your way out of this Judgement verdict? Explain.

11. Revelation 20:15, What will these people's punishment be?

Will All Christians Go to Heaven?

Some people believe that if they say they are a Christian they will automatically go to heaven when they die. I am sorry to inform them that this is not the case, only real Christians go to heaven.

> Not every one that saith unto me, Lord, Lord, shall enter into the kingdom of heaven; but he that doeth the will of my Father which is in heaven.
> Matthew 7:21

The above verse is referring to people with outward appearances of salvation, but never accepted salvation in their hearts. This type of person is usually called a professing Christian. They professed with their mouth but not with their hearts. Many believe that God only looks at their works, but a real Christian knows God looks at our hearts.

A professing Christian usually believes they can work or buy their way to heaven. The Bible says this is not possible.

> For by **grace** are ye saved **through faith**; and that **not of yourselves**: it is the gift of God: [9] **Not of works**, lest any man should boast.
> Ephesians 2:8-9

> Jesus saith unto him, I am the way, the truth, and the life: **no man cometh unto the Father, but by me**.
> John 14:6

A Christian will try their very best to be Christ-like. They will stumble but continue to try their best to live like Christ. Some professing Christians do not. They go to church on Sunday and play their role as super Christian then on Monday they go back to their sinful ways and see nothing wrong in doing so.

> They profess that they know God; but in works they deny him, being abominable, and disobedient, and unto every good work reprobate.
> Titus 1:16

How will we know if someone is a professing Christian or a true Christian? The answer is we will not always know. We might feel that something is not right, but we do not know for sure. But God knows and I believe they know also. Christianity has become a game or a show to them.

They appear to have everything under control, but it is all a public act. God's word also tells us not to judge others.

One might ask, how do I know for sure I am not a professing Christian, and I am going to Heaven when I die? The answer is VERY simple. When you accepted Jesus as you Savor did you mean it? Do you believe he died on the cross, was buried, and rose again? Do you believe Jesus is God's son born from a virgin birth? Do you believe the Bible is God's word? If you do not, please search your heart and make it right today.

> For God so loved the world, that he gave his only begotten Son, that whosoever believeth in him should not perish, but have everlasting life. 17 For God sent not his Son into the world to condemn the world; but *that the world through him might be saved*.
> John 3:16-17

Heaven and End Times

1. Matthew 7:21, In your own words explain what this verse means.

2. Ephesians 2:8-9, John 14:6, Can you work your way to Heaven? Explain.

3. Philippians 3:8, Isaiah 64:6, What does the Bible call our righteousness without Jesus?

4. Titus 1:16, Is it possible to profess that you are a Christian and even do good deeds, but not be allowed into Heaven? Explain.

5. Matthew 7:20, Matthew 12:33, James 3:12, We cannot judge others and know for sure if they are playing church or are saved, but what are some of the signs?

6. How do you know for sure you are not a professing Christian?

7. John 14:6, What is the only way to Heaven?

8. Revelation 21:27, Can sin enter Heaven? Explain.

9. John 3:17, 2 Corinthians 5:21, Jesus was not sent to this world to condemn us but to _____ us? What did he do to save us?

10. Will all Christians go to Heaven? Think carefully.

Firstfruits

Firstfruits are the very first of everything created. God instructed the Hebrews to give these firstfruits to God because he is the creator of everything and therefore, they belong to him. This even applied to humans,

> The earth is the Lord's, and the fulness thereof; the world, and they that dwell therein.
> Psalm 24:1

We as Christians are also considered firstfruit upon accepting Jesus as our Savior. At this point, we become indwelled by the Holy Spirit and obtain a promise of a future blessing.

> And **not only they, but ourselves also, which have the firstfruits of the Spirit,** even we ourselves groan within ourselves, waiting for the adoption, to wit, the redemption of our body.
> Romans 8:23
>
> Of his own will begat he us with the word of truth, that we should **be a kind of firstfruits of his creatures**.
> James 1:18

I believe "A kind of firstfruits" means that those who accept Jesus as their Savior need not give a firstfruit offering as they are indwelled with the Holy Spirit and are themselves a firstfruit. As a firstfruit, we should take care of our body as it is a temple to help Jesus reach others with the gospel.

> I beseech you therefore, brethren, by the mercies of God, that ye present your bodies a living sacrifice, holy, acceptable unto God, which is your reasonable service.
> Romans 12:1

The biggest proof that Christians do not have to give firstfruit offerings is that Jesus fulfilled this law. Jesus, although crucified on the cross and buried, did not die. Because of him, we have hope of everlasting life with him. He is indeed the firstfruit over death and if you note in Corinthians it says, "afterward they that are Christ's". This means those who accept him as their Savior.

> *But now is Christ risen from the dead, and become **the firstfruits** of them that slept. 23 But every man in his own order: **Christ the firstfruits**; afterward they that are Christ's at his coming.*
> *1Corinthians 15:20,23*

> And he is the head of the body, the church: who is the beginning, ***the firstborn from the dead***; that in all things he might have the preeminence (surpassing all others).
> Colossians 1:18

Although Christians do not have to give firstfruit offerings we are expected to give ten percent of everything to God in tithes. Tithes are the means for the modern church to finance the running of the church and its man of God. The only reason I mention tithes is that some preach firstfruit offerings above and beyond tithes and offerings with the promise that if you do so you will prosper. For instance, your whole first paycheck of the year could be considered a firstfruit offering. This is called prosperity preaching and is not biblical. What they are saying is, you make me rich, and God will make you rich.

Revelation tells us of 144,000 Jews who are saved, sealed, and protected by God during the Tribulation. They are considered Christians and called firstfruits as were Christians after the first coming of Christ. They will serve God but no mention of an offering other than themselves,

> These are they which were not defiled with women; for they are virgins. These are they which follow the Lamb whithersoever he goeth. These were redeemed from among men, being the **firstfruits** unto God and to the Lamb.
> Revelation 14:4

In conclusion, to be a Firstfruit of Christ one must accept Jesus as their Savior. We know from previous studies that those not found in the Lambs book of life will not be allowed in Heaven. Therefore, only Firstfruits of Christ will enter Heaven. So, I encourage you to examine yourself and know for sure you are a firstfruit of Jesus.

1. Exodus 22:29-31, Exodus 13:1-2, How would you define firstfruit?

2. Exodus 22:29, Hints of firstborn child sacrifice, but Exodus 13:8 shows us the true meaning. What is the firstborn purpose at this festival?

3. Deuteronomy 18:10, Deuteronomy 12:31, Does God condone human sacrifice?

4. James 1:18, What do you believe a kind of firstfruits means?

5. Romans 12:1, 1 Corinthians 6:19, Ephesians 5:27, Should we take care of our bodies as a firstfruit of God?

6. 1 Corinthians 15:20,23 and Colossians 1:18, What does it mean that Jesus is the firstfruits over the dead?

7. According to the verses in question 6, how does that make Christians also firstfruits over death?

8. Revelation 14:4, Do you see anywhere that these firstfruits had to make a firstfruit offering?

9. Could it be that the reason firstfruit humans do not have to give a firstfruit offering is that we are the offering? That our offering is our service to God?

Rewards and Crowns of Heaven?

We all perceive things differently. When my husband and I first started dating he talked of groundhog hunting. I told him I had never seen a groundhog before. This statement shocked him as I am from a small country area in the Catskill Mountains. So, he laughingly invited me on a trip to his favorite hunting grounds. On our way, a critter crossed the road in front of us and he looked at me and said, "that is a groundhog". I giggled and said, "We call them woodchucks, where I come from".

So, why am I telling you a story from my life? I am just using it as an object lesson to show that something you see one way does not necessarily mean someone else will see it or call it the same way, but it is. My husband is from West Virginia and I am from New York. It was the same animal only with a different regional name.

Not only might we not see things the same way, but the level of importance or value of something can be viewed differently. I might think my home is a mansion and worth way more than its true value and you might view it as a shack.

From what I can gather, five crowns can be earned while living in our human form on earth. I have seen people list up to thirteen possible crowns, but they all come under one of the five crowns' meanings. The crown(s) are our reward for what we have done for God. We can earn more than one crown based on our faithfulness and service to God. It all depends on how we perceive rewards and what value we put on them.

What are these five crowns? They are:
1. Incorruptible
2. Rejoicing
3. Righteousness
4. Life
5. Glory

THE INCORRUPTIBLE CROWN is awarded to those who live a Godly life on earth. They are wholly serving God, putting him before themselves. They not only try to stay away from sinful things but also are not distracted by the world. They are shining examples instead of distractions. They will be victorious over the world.

> And every man that striveth for the mastery is temperate in all things. Now they do it to obtain a corruptible crown; but we an

incorruptible. [26] I therefore so run, not as uncertainly; so fight I, not as one that beateth the air: [27] But I keep under my body, and bring it into subjection: lest that by any means, when I have preached to others, I myself should be a castaway.

1 Corinthians 9:25-27

THE CROWN OF REJOICING is sometimes called the Soul-Winner's Crown. It is given to those who earnestly share the plan of Salvation with others so they too can go to heaven.

> For what is our hope, or joy, or crown of rejoicing? Are not even ye in the presence of our Lord Jesus Christ at his coming?
>
> 1 Thessalonians 2:19

THE CROWN OF RIGHTEOUSNESS is the crown for those who truly long for heaven and to see the face of Jesus. I must admit I struggle with this one because I am weak. It is not because I do not want to go to heaven or see Jesus' face, because I do. But I think of the pain my passing would inflict on others and how I love being with my loved ones.

I discussed this dilemma with my husband because my feelings deeply disturbed me. After talking to him I felt much better. He said, "I do not want to die today but I am not afraid of dying and at the appropriate time I look forward to seeing Jesus in person." I then realized that longing for Jesus does not necessarily mean rushing Jesus.

> A time to be born, and a time to die; a time to plant, and a time to pluck up that which is planted;
>
> Ecclesiastes 3:2

Sometimes I feel unchristian when I hear others say, "Come today Lord Jesus" and I am thinking, "I hope not because there are so many unsaved family members and friends". I must also admit that sometimes I wonder if they truly mean what they say. But it is not for me to judge if these people truly mean these words, or if they say them for appearance's sake. I hope they truly mean them because it will be a great crown to earn.

> Henceforth there is laid up for me a crown of righteousness, which the Lord, the righteous judge, shall give me at that day: and not to me only, but unto all them also that love his appearing.
>
> 2 Timothy 4:8

THE CROWN OF LIFE is for the persecuted. When we think of persecution, we think of people who die in martyrdom for Jesus' sake. But it is also for those who by keeping their faith are caused to lose things dear to them like family, friends, jobs, etc. In other words, people who have suffered for the Gospel.

> Blessed is the man that endureth temptation: for when he is tried, he shall receive the crown of life, which the Lord hath promised to them that love him.
>
> James 1:12

> Fear none of those things which thou shalt suffer: behold, the devil shall cast some of you into prison, that ye may be tried; and ye shall have Tribulation ten days: be thou faithful unto death, and I will give thee a crown of life.
>
> Revelation 2:10

THE CROWN OF GLORY is for those who shepherd God's people. It is not a reward just for pastors but includes those faithful in shepherding which includes elders, deacons, Sunday school teachers, ministry team leaders, youth group leaders, etc.

> The elders which are among you I exhort, who am also an elder, and a witness of the sufferings of Christ, and also a partaker of the glory that shall be revealed: ² Feed the flock of God which is among you, taking the oversight thereof, not by constraint, but willingly; not for filthy lucre, but of a ready mind; ³ Neither as being lords over God's heritage, but being examples to the flock. ⁴ And when the chief Shepherd shall appear, ye shall receive a crown of glory that fadeth not away.
>
> 1 Peter 5:1-4

How do you perceive these crowns? Are they valuable to you? Or, do you think fire insurance is enough? Someday we will all find out.

1. According to this lesson, what are the five crowns Christians can receive in Heaven?

2. 1 Corinthians 9:25-27, What is the qualification for Victor's Crown?

3. 1 Thessalonians 2:19, Why do you think it is called a Crown of Rejoicing?

4. 2 Timothy 4:8, What crown do we have here and how does one obtain it?

5. James 1:12, Revelation 2:10, What is the name of this crown? How does one obtain this crown? Do you have to be murdered to receive this crown? Explain.

6. 1 Peter 5:1-4, What is the name of this reward? Who are eligible for this reward?

7. What are the duties of a church leader to be considered for the crown of glory?

8. Can you acquire more than one crown? Explain.

9. Are we all going to receive the same crowns?

Are There Different Levels of Heaven?

We all know that the Bible speaks of three heavens. They consist of the air that we breathe, outer space, and Heaven where God lives. But are there different levels in the Heaven that God lives in?

The Bible does not say anything about there being different levels in Heaven. There are however different non-Christian religions that do. Hinduism and ancient Babylonians are two of these religions.

Hinduism teaches there are seven higher worlds where people with good karma go and seven lower worlds where the people with bad karma go after death.

Ancient Babylonians taught that there are seven levels of heaven between earth and heaven which were based on the moon, sun, and five planets (Mercury, Venus, Mars, Jupiter, and Saturn).

The Bible does talk about different levels of rewards which can confuse some to think that our rewards earn us a place in a higher level of Heaven.

We know that when we as Christians die, we will be judged by what we have done for God on Earth. We will not lose our place in Heaven for disappointing God because Jesus died for all who believe and call upon His name.

> Every man's work shall be made manifest: for the day shall declare it, because it shall be revealed by fire; and the fire shall try every man's work of what sort it is.[14] If any man's work abide which he hath built thereupon, he shall receive a ***reward***.[15] If any man's work shall be burned, **he shall suffer loss: but he himself shall be saved**; yet so as by fire.
>
> 1 Corinthians 3:13-15

Jesus often used parables (relatable stories) to teach. One of these parables is a story about the kingdom of heaven compared to a traveling man who gave his servants talents to invest for him while he was gone. To one he gave five, another two, and one he gave one. All doubled their talents except the one with one talent,

> But he that had received one went and digged in the earth, and hid his lord's money.
>
> Matthew 25:18

The one who was given 5 talents,

> His lord said unto him, Well done, thou good and faithful servant: thou hast been faithful over a few things, ***I will make thee ruler over many things***: enter thou into the joy of thy lord.
> Matthew 25:21

The one who was given two talents,

> His lord said unto him, Well done, good and faithful servant; thou hast been faithful over a few things, ***I will make thee ruler over many things***: enter thou into the joy of thy lord.
> Matthew 25:23

We all should want to hear well done thy good and faithful son, however, the one with one talent buried his and did not.

> His lord answered and said unto him, Thou wicked and slothful servant, thou knewest that I reap where I sowed not, and gather where I have not strawed:..[28] Take therefore the talent from him, and give it unto him which hath ten talents.[29] For unto every one that hath shall be given, and he shall have abundance: but from him that hath not shall be taken away even that which he hath.
> Matthew 25: 26,28-29

Whoa, wait a minute, did I not say earlier that we could not lose our salvation? Do not worry, we will not lose it. Jesus knew this man was not saved to start with. One cannot lose what they never possessed.

Although we will be rewarded for our service to God our greatest reward will be our inheritance into the family of God.

> And whatsoever ye do, do it heartily, as to the Lord, and not unto men;[24] Knowing that of the Lord ye shall receive the reward of the **inheritance**: for ye serve the Lord Christ.
> Colossians 3:23-24

The rewards given in heaven will be precious to us because they reflect the end of our earthly lives and in our heavenly lives, we will share them with Jesus. Yes, some will bear more rewards than others. Some will be over more heavenly projects than others. But no one will be jealous because each will realize they could have done more for God than was done. We might be sad and ashamed because we did not, but we will not be loved any less. There will not be a naughty or nice level in Heaven.

Heaven and End Times

1. 1 Corinthians 3:13-15, How will deeds be tried?

2. 1 Corinthians 3:13-15, If we do not get any rewards in Heaven, will we lose our place and not go to Heaven? Explain.

3. Colossians 3:23-24, Romans 8:16-17, What will be our greatest reward?

4. Matthew 25:21, 23, What are the words every Christian should want to hear?

5. According to Matthew 25:21, 23, Will we have various positions of authority in Heaven? Explain.

6. Matthew 25:28-29, This man's reward was taken away, does that mean we can lose our salvation? Look closely at verse 29. Explain.

7. Matthew 20:1-16, Does it matter how long you have been a Christian to be treated equally and enter Heaven? Explain.

8. Some believe there are different levels of Heaven where the good is at a higher level and the naughty live on the bottom level. Do you think this is true? Explain.

Four Heavens?

Are there four Heavens? If so, are they the same or different, and what are their purposes? Where is the home of God now? Can they be found in the Bible? These are all things that baffle our minds.

We know that there is more than one heaven because of verses that mention Heavens.

> Seeing then that we have a great high priest, that is passed into the **heavens**, Jesus the Son of God, let us hold fast our profession.
> Hebrews 4:14

> Thou, even thou, art Lord alone; thou hast made heaven, the heaven of **heavens**, with all their host, the earth, and all things that are therein, the seas, and all that is therein, and thou preservest them all; and the host of heaven worshippeth thee.
> Nehemiah 9:6

We have now established that there is more than one heaven. So, are there four Heavens? The answer is yes, although one is still being prepared. Let us break them down.

First Heaven: We live in the first heaven. The Bible tells us that God created this on the second day and that birds fly in this heaven. We know that birds would die if let loose into outer space. We also know that it does not rain in outer space.

> And God made the firmament, and divided the waters which were under the firmament from the waters which were above the firmament: and it was so. 8 And God called the firmament Heaven. And the evening and the morning were the second day…[20]And God said, Let the waters bring forth abundantly the moving creature that hath life, and *fowl that may fly above the earth in the open firmament of heaven.*
> Genesis 1:7-8,20

> And he prayed again, and *the heaven gave rain*, and the earth brought forth her fruit.
> James 5:18

Second Heaven: Not only does the second heaven hold the sun, moon, and stars to separate the day from night, but it was made to show us the glory of God, to provide signs and seasons.

> The heavens declare the glory of God; and the firmament sheweth his handywork. ² Day unto day uttereth speech, and night unto night sheweth knowledge.
> Psalm 19:1-2

> And God said, Let there be lights in the firmament of the heaven to divide the day from the night; and let them be for signs, and for seasons, and for days, and years: ¹⁵ And let them be for lights in the firmament of the heaven to give light upon the earth: and it was so. ¹⁶ And God made two great lights; the greater light to rule the day, and the lesser light to rule the night: he made the stars also. ¹⁷ And God set them in the firmament of the heaven to give light upon the earth, ¹⁸ And to rule over the day and over the night, and to divide the light from the darkness: and God saw that it was good.
> Genesis 1:14-18

Third Heaven: The third Heaven is where God currently lives and rules from.

> I knew a man in Christ above fourteen years ago, (whether in the body, I cannot tell; or whether out of the body, I cannot tell: God knoweth;) such an one caught up to the ***third heaven.***
> 2 Corinthians 12:2

> And lest thou lift up thine eyes unto heaven, and when thou seest the sun, and the moon, and the stars, even all the host of heaven, shouldest be driven to worship them, and serve them, which the Lord thy God hath divided unto all nations ***under the <u>whole</u> heaven***.
> Deuteronomy 4:19

Fourth Heaven: The fourth Heaven is called the New Jerusalem. It is the Heaven that all Christians will live in for eternity. Our present earth and air will be replaced by it. This new Jerusalem is still under construction as far as we know.

> And I saw a new heaven and a new earth: for ***the first heaven and the first earth were passed away***; and there was no more sea. 2 And I John saw the ***holy city, new Jerusalem***, coming down from God out of heaven, prepared as a bride adorned for her husband. 3 And I heard a great voice out of heaven saying, Behold, the tabernacle of God is with men, and he will dwell with them, and they shall be his people, and God himself shall be with them, and be their God.
> Revelation 21:1-3

> Let not your heart be troubled: ye believe in God, believe also in me. 2 In my Father's house are many mansions: if it were not so, I would have told you. I go to prepare a place for you. 3 And if I go and prepare a place for you, I will come again, and receive you unto myself; that where I am, there ye may be also.
>
> John 14:1-3

God resides in Heaven which is described as north. I believe the term north is used because in our mind's north is always up and the south is down. Job tells us the earth is in an empty place. Even in his days, they realized that this could not be if God had not made it so. This empty place is our universe.

> He stretcheth out the **north** over the *empty place*, and ***hangeth the earth upon nothing.***
>
> Job 26:7

We are also told that God came down which would be the reverse of us going up to heaven. It makes sense that the first heaven is our atmosphere, the second outer space (universe), and the third heaven would be above the first two or in other words, north.

> Go to, **let us go down**, and there confound their language, that they may not understand one another's speech.
>
> Genesis 11:7

I have provided you with Bible verses to verify that all this is indeed found in the Bible. I challenge you to do a more in-depth study of your own.

Heaven and End Times

1. Hebrews 4:14, Nehemiah 9:6, Is there more than one heaven in the Bible? Explain your answer.

2. Genesis 1:7-8, Who divided the waters?

3. Genesis 1:7-8, What did God call the firmament above the waters?

4. Genesis 1:7-8, James 5:18, Where is the first heaven located? Explain.

5. Psalm 148:3-6, Psalm 19:1-2, Genesis 1:14-18, Where is the second heaven and what is found in the second heaven?

6. 2 Corinthians 12:2, Deuteronomy 4:19, States that there is a _____ Heaven and it is located where?

7. Job 26:7, The empty place is our universe and earth hangs on nothing. What direction is Heaven located from earth?

8. Genesis 11:7, Where is God talking of going?

9. Genesis 11:7, Which direction was God talking of going?

10. Genesis 11:7, So what conclusion can you draw for the direction of Heaven?

11. Revelation 21:1-3, After Jesus returns what will God make?

12. What will the new Heaven be called?

13. Revelation 21:3, Does this mean that the new Jerusalem and earth will be the new Heaven? Explain.

14. John 14:1-3, How do we know Christians will be in this new Heaven?

Even Heaven Has Walls! But, Maybe Not For The Reason You Think!

Walls have many functions. They keep trespassers out, keep animals in, or are decorative. In Bible times, they surrounded cities and were used for protection from rivals or enemies.

Protection
- Everyone has heard of the Bible story about the walls of Jericho. The walls of Jericho were massive. I never realized that the dimensions included three tiers of walls. I always imagined it was called the walls of Jericho because it had four sides and surrounded Jericho. Very interesting, but a study for another time. This new information just makes the story even more meaningful to me because God allowed Joshua to bring them tumbling down. Wow! Even though the walls were extremely thick and tall, they could not protect the people from God.

Keep animals in
- The sheepfold is where sheep were kept at night to protect them from thieves and predators. You are probably familiar with this passage:

> Verily, verily, I say unto you, He that entereth not by the door into the sheepfold, but climbeth up some other way, the same is a thief and a robber.
>
> John 10:1

Sheepfold walls are interesting. I found that there were different types of sheepfolds, but for the most part, they consisted of loosely stacked stones. Check out this website, it is very interesting.
http://www.Bible-history.com/sketches/ancient/sheep-fold.html

Decorative
- This is the category I believe the walls of New Jerusalem (Heaven) fall into. The Bible tells us we will not need the sun or moon for light. God's glory will provide all the light we need.

> And the city had no need of the sun, neither of the moon, to shine in it: for the glory of God did lighten it, and the Lamb is the light thereof. 24 And the nations of them which are saved shall walk in the light of it: and the kings of the earth do bring their glory and

honour into it. 25 And the **gates of it shall not be shut at all by day: for there shall be no night there.**

Revelation 21:23-25

With this in mind let us look at the walls of heaven, which gates are open all the time. If they are opened all the time, then the walls were not built for protection or to keep something in, ***but for beauty***.

I believe that God's glory shines through the precious stones of the walls and magnifies outwards all the beautiful colors of the walls. Think about it, light shining through 200 feet thick walls made of precious stones.

As a child, I was fascinated with kaleidoscopes. I remember being mesmerized by all the beautiful colors. I am positive that Heaven's walls will be even more beautiful than anyone can imagine.

The wall itself is Jasper. The foundation is garnished with precious stones and according to Revelation 21:12-14, the walls hold the names of the twelve apostles of Jesus and the gates the names of the twelve tribes of Israel. So, what are the precious stones that make up Heaven's walls? I prepared a list of them below. Remember Heaven will be made of pure elements, so go with the pure colors.

LIST OF STONES FOUND IN REVELATION 21:18-20

1. Jasper- Red, yellow, brown mixture (today's birthstone dark green with red bands)
2. Sapphire-in biblical times it was said to be blue of the sky, shining brightly with gold specks
3. Chalcedony- milky white, light gray, blue, and yellowish-brown
4. Emerald-Grassy green
5. Sardonyx-has alternating bands of reddish-brown and white
6. Sardius- orangish-red
7. Chrysolyte-Yellow/green
8. Beryl-Blue/green often likened to the color of the sea
9. Topaz-golden colored
10. Chrysoprasus-translucent, bright apple green
11. Jacinth-diluted blue/violet color
12. Amethyst-rich, violet-purple color

Not only are the walls made of precious stones, but the twelve gates are each made of one pearl.

> And the twelve gates were twelve pearls: every several gate was of one pearl:
>
> Revelation 21:21a

I do not know about you, but I am looking forward to seeing all these beautiful colors shining everywhere. The walls themselves will be more beautiful than anything we have seen on earth. Heaven is indeed a perk of knowing Jesus! Mediate this week on the walls of Heaven and their beauty? Are you looking forward to seeing them?

Heaven and End Times

1. Joshua 6:1, 20, What were these walls made for?

2. John 10:1, Numbers 32:16, What are these walls made for?

3. Revelation 21:23-25, What is the only light in Heaven?

4. Revelation 21:25, What do you think these walls are for if the gates are never shut?

5. Revelation 21:12, How many gates are there?

6. Revelation 21:12, What is written on the Gates?

7. Revelation 21:14, What is written on the foundation of the wall?

8. Revelation 21:21, What are the gates made of?

9. Revelation 21:18, What is the wall made of?

10. Revelation 21:19-20, Name the stones that are garnishing the foundations of the wall.

1. _____	2. _____	3. _____
4. _____	5. _____	6. _____
7. _____	8. _____	9. _____
10. _____	11. _____	12. _____

11. Revelation 21:27, Who are the only people that will be allowed to enter or leave this new Jerusalem?

Will we know each other in Heaven?

Will we know each other in Heaven is a question that lingers in all our minds. Many scholars say no, I believe yes. I will report, and you can decide for yourself.

Jesus himself often made references to people knowing one and another:

> But I say unto you, I will not drink henceforth of this fruit of the vine, **until that day when I drink it new with you in my Father's kingdom.**
>
> Matthew 26:29

> And I say unto you, That many shall come from the east and west, and **shall sit down with Abraham, and Isaac, and Jacob, in the kingdom of heaven.**
>
> Matthew 8:11

> And was transfigured before them: and his face did shine as the sun, and his raiment was white as the light.[3] And, behold, **there appeared unto them Moses and Elias talking with him.**
>
> Matthew 17:2-3

The Bible tells us of the story of Lazarus and the rich man. Lazarus was very poor, covered in sores, and ate crumbs from beneath the rich man's table. Lazarus died and was taken by angels to Abraham's bosom. When the rich man died, he went to hell. From there he saw Abraham and Lazarus in Abraham's bosom (the heavenly holding place for those who were heaven-bound before the death of Jesus).

> And in hell he lift up his eyes, being in torments, and seeth Abraham afar off, and Lazarus in his bosom.
>
> Luke 16:23

We know that our names must be in the book of life for us to enter Heaven vs the Lake of Fire. Our names being listed in this book hints that we will keep our identity in heaven.

> but rather rejoice, because your names are written in heaven.
>
> Luke 10:20b

David tells us in 2 Samuel that his son cannot return to him, but he will go to him someday.

> But now he is dead, wherefore should I fast? can I bring him back again? I shall go to him, but he shall not return to me.
>
> 2 Samuel 12:23

Paul comforted people who lost loved ones with these words,

> That ye may walk honestly toward them that are without, and that ye may have lack of nothing.13 But I *would not have you to be ignorant, brethren, concerning them which are asleep, that ye sorrow not, even as others which have no hope*. 14 For if we believe that Jesus died and rose again, even so them also which sleep in Jesus will God bring with him. 15 For this we say unto you by the word of the Lord, that we which are alive and remain unto the coming of the Lord shall not prevent them which are asleep. 16 *For the Lord himself shall descend from heaven with a shout, with the voice of the archangel, and with the trump of God: and the dead in Christ shall rise first: 17 Then we which are alive and remain shall be caught up together with them in the clouds*, to meet the Lord in the air: and so shall we ever be with the Lord. 18 Wherefore *comfort one another with these words*.
>
> 1 Thessalonians 4:12-18

The Sadducees questioned Jesus about a woman that was married seven times. They wanted to know who her husband would be in heaven. Jesus answered that it was more important to know God than to worry about what heaven would be like. In other words, do not try to put earthly limitations on Heaven. He went on to say,

> for in the resurrection they neither marry, nor are given in marriage, but are as the angels of God in heaven.
>
> Matthew 22:30

I take this verse to mean that we will know each other but we will not have sexual desires or feelings of jealousy. We will not be angels but just like angels, we will not reproduce. We will feel love for each other, and our goal will be to serve God only.

We will be given new names, but I believe that our names will not change knowing each other. So, then why are we given new names on white stones?

> He that hath an ear, let him hear what the Spirit saith unto the churches; To him that overcometh will I give to eat of the hidden

manna, ***and will give him a white stone, and in the stone a new name written, which no man knoweth saving he that receiveth it.***
Revelation 2:17

Many times, in the Bible, God changed people's names; Abraham, Paul, Sarah are prime examples. Their names were changed by God because they had a change of heart or achieved higher godly characteristics etc. But after their names were changed everyone still knew who they were. Our new name will be a special bond between God and us. Our name will reflect the growth, and sacrifices we made for Christ.

I believe the white stone means we are forgiven. In the early Roman courts of the Bible, white stones were cast to acquit someone, and black stones were cast for a judgement of guilt.

In conclusion, I believe we will know each other and that God will declare us righteous and our new names will reflex our earthly life. But if I am wrong it will not matter because we will be happy just to be with Jesus and God.

Heaven and End Times

1. Matthew 17:2-3, Matthew 8:11, Matthew 26:29, Are these verses saying we will recognize people? List the personal references that you see.

2, Luke 16:22, Where was Lazarus taken?

3. Luke 16:22-23, Where was the rich man taken?

4. Luke 10:20, What is listed in heaven?

5. 2 Samuel 12:23, David said that he could not bring his son back, but he would _____?

6. 1 Thessalonians 4:16-17, Who will Jesus meet in the air?

7. Matthew 22:30, After we die, no one will get married. Does this make us angels or just similar to angels?

8. Hebrews 1:14, Who are the angels' ministers to?

9. 2 Peter 2:4, Is talking about what?

10. 1 Corinthians 13:12, Pay special attention to the last part of this verse. Do you believe it means we will know each other? Explain.

11. Revelation 2:17, Do you believe that others will still know you even with a new name?

What Will Heaven Look Like?

One thing all Christians look forward to is the promise of living with Jesus in Heaven. Have you ever wondered what heaven will look like? Will it be ordinary like our world or something spectacular? Are the streets made of gold? Are Heaven and the New Jerusalem both the same?

I believe heaven's beauty will be beyond our human comprehension. The beautiful 200 ft thick wall of jasper with its foundation of twelve different layers of beautiful stones already has me envisioning the majesty of God's light shining through it. If the wall does not intrigue you, what about the city itself which will be made of pure clear gold?

> And the building of the wall of it was of jasper: and ***the city was pure gold, like unto clear glass.*** [19] And the foundations of the wall of the city were garnished with all manner of precious stones. The first foundation was jasper; the second, sapphire; the third, a chalcedony; the fourth, an emerald; [20] The fifth, sardonyx; the sixth, sardius; the seventh, chrysolyte; the eighth, beryl; the ninth, a topaz; the tenth, a chrysoprasus; the eleventh, a jacinth; the twelfth, an amethyst.
>
> Revelation 21:18-20

Not only are the twelve walls of heaven made of jasper with twelve different layers of precious stones, but each gate is made of one massive pearl. As humans, we have trouble fathoming that each gate could consist of one giant pearl.

> And had a wall great and high, and had twelve gates, and at the gates twelve angels, and names written thereon, which are the names of the twelve tribes of the children of Israel: 13 On the east three gates; on the north three gates; on the south three gates; and on the west three gates... 21 ***And the twelve gates were twelve pearls: every several gate was of one pearl:***
>
> Revelation 21:12-13, 21a

Will the streets be made of gold? The answer is yes!

> and the street of the city was pure gold, as it were transparent glass.
>
> Revelation 21:21b

Heaven and End Times

There will be no darkness there for the glory of God will light Heaven through Jesus.

> And the city had no need of the sun, neither of the moon, to shine in it: for ***the glory of God did lighten it, and the Lamb is the light thereof.*** 24 And the nations of them which are saved shall walk in the light of it: and the kings of the earth do bring their glory and honour into it. 25 And the gates of it shall not be shut at all by day: for there shall be no night there.
> Revelation 21:23-25

On top of all the other beauty described, there will be a river flowing from the throne of God and Jesus. The water of this river will be so pure that it will look like crystal. The tree of life will be on both sides of this river. It will bear twelve different fruits.

> And he shewed me a ***pure river of water of life, clear as crystal***, proceeding out of the throne of God and of the Lamb. ² In the midst of the street of it, and ***on either side of the river, was there the tree of life***, which bare twelve manner of fruits, and yielded her fruit every month: and the leaves of the tree were for the healing of the nations.
> Revelation 22:1-2

Although Heaven is made to be pleasing to our eyes, the most beautiful and reverent beauty will be God and His throne. I can see in my mind the beauty that illuminates from God, the rainbow surrounding his throne, and the lightning and thunder that radiates from it. Later we will study what Revelation four means. But for now, we are just looking into the beauty of heaven.

> After this I looked, and, behold, a door was opened in heaven: and the first voice which I heard was as it were of a trumpet talking with me; which said, Come up hither, and I will shew thee things which must be hereafter. ² And immediately I was in the spirit: and, behold, a throne was set in heaven, and one sat on the throne. ³ And he that sat was to look upon like a jasper and a sardine stone: and there was a rainbow round about the throne, in sight like unto an emerald. ⁴ And round about the throne were four and twenty seats: and upon the seats I saw four and twenty elders sitting, clothed in white raiment; and they had on their heads crowns of gold. ⁵ And out of the throne proceeded lightnings and thunderings and voices: and there were seven lamps of fire burning before the throne, which are the seven Spirits of God.
> Revelation 4:1-5

After the millennial reign of Christ, there will be a battle of Gog and Magog which we will study later. God will defeat these armies with fire from Heaven and cast Satan into the Lake of Fire. There will then be the final judgement of all who did not accept Jesus as their Saviour and they too will be tossed into the Lake of Fire. Following this, the Bible tells us the old earth and old heaven will be destroyed and a new earth and heaven will be made. It is believed that the heaven that will be destroyed is our atmosphere, not the Heaven God lives in. Our atmosphere has been marred by the past presence of Satan and evil spirits. The new Heaven that surrounds the earth will be pure of any sin. But even if all Heavens are destroyed, I believe that the New Jerusalem is already the place that God dwells in Heaven. It comes down to earth:

> And I John saw the holy city, new Jerusalem, coming down from God out of heaven, prepared as a bride adorned for her husband.
> Revelation 21:2

The New Jerusalem (God's Home) will now be located on earth. It will replace the current corrupt capital of God's people. We will worship God there. He will be our God and we will be his people.

The Bible gives us the size of the New Jerusalem, but it does not tell us the size of the new earth. We do know there will be no sea. The New Jerusalem itself will be a fifteen-hundred-mile square cube, enough to house billions of people.

> And he that talked with me had a golden reed to measure the city, and the gates thereof, and the wall thereof. [16] And the city lieth foursquare, and the length is as large as the breadth: and he measured the city with the reed, twelve thousand furlongs. The length and the breadth and the height of it are equal. [17] And he measured the wall thereof, an hundred and forty and four cubits, according to the measure of a man, that is, of the angel.
> Revelation 21:15-17

With that said, all we need to know is that the new earth and heaven will be big enough to house all those who have accepted Jesus as their Saviour. I believe that since there is an earth and the twelve gates of New Jerusalem (Heaven) are never closed, some will live and work outside of the walls of the New Jerusalem. I base this on the fact that nations walk in the light of

New Jerusalem and kings bring glory and honor into it. Also, your name must be written into the book of life to enter.

> And the **nations** of them which are saved shall **walk in the light of it**: and the **kings of the earth do bring their glory and honour <u>into</u> it**.
> Revelation 21:24
> And there shall in no wise enter into it any thing that defileth, neither whatsoever worketh abomination, or maketh a lie: **but they which are written in the Lamb's book of life.**
> Revelation 21:27

In Conclusion, Heaven will indeed be the most beautiful place we will ever see, but there is only one way to achieve the honor of living forever there and viewing this marvelous place every day. That is by accepting Jesus Christ as your savior.

Have you asked Jesus into your heart? If you are not sure, please search the word of God (Bible) for directions or seek a local Pastor or Christian to help lead you to the saving grace of God.

1. Revelation 21:18, What will the city of the new Jerusalem be made of?

2. Revelation 21:21, What will the streets of Heaven be made of?

3. Revelation 21:23-25, Will there be darkness in Heaven? Explain your answer.

4. Revelation 21:16, Gives the measurement of 12,000 furlongs (A furlong is 660'). 12,000 x 660' = 7,920,000' ÷ 5,280' (ft in a mile) = 1500 miles. Therefore, the new Jerusalem will be a _____ square mile cube.

5. Revelation 4:3, What does God's throne look like?

6. Exodus 33:18, What did Moses ask God to show him?

7. Exodus 33:20, What does God say about humans looking upon his Glory?

8. Exodus 33:22, What does God do for Moses?

9. Exodus 34:29-35, After the brief contact with God, what happened to Moses' face and what did he have to do to calm the people's fears?

10. Revelation 4:3, Says that he who sat on the throne looked like Jasper and sardine stone. We know we cannot look at God while we are human. John was still human. Do you think that God used the reflection of colors around him to protect John as he had Moses?

11. Acts 22:11-13, Just a slight glance at the glory of Jesus did what to Paul?

12. Revelation 4:3, What color is the rainbow around God's throne?

13. Revelation 4:5, What is seen and heard coming from the throne?

14. Revelation 21:23-24, Do you think people will also live outside of the New Jerusalem? Explain.

God's Throne in Heaven

God's throne is not only a thing of beauty but a statement of power.

Imagine the beauty of God illuminating as jasper and sardine stone. The Jasper spoken of in the Bible was usually red, brown, or yellow combinations, and sardine was blood red to an orangish-red color, obtained from Sardis in Lydia. This sight alone would be a wonder of beauty, but then add a rainbow around the throne that appeared as emerald (which are usually lightish green in color).

> And he that sat was to look upon like a jasper and a sardine stone: and there was a rainbow round about the throne, in sight like unto an emerald.
>
> Revelation 4:3

To add to this beauty is the sight of seven lamps of fire burning before the throne. Some refer to this as the seven spirits of God. We know these seven spirits as being all rolled into one, which we call the Holy Spirit.

> and there were seven lamps of fire burning before the throne, which are the seven Spirits of God.
>
> Revelation 4:5b

Before you go bonkers trying to figure out what the seven spirits are that make up the Holy Spirit, they are found in Isaiah:

> And the spirit of the **Lord** shall rest upon him, the spirit of **wisdom** and **understanding**, the spirit of **counsel** and **might**, the spirit of **knowledge** and of the **fear** (respect) of the Lord;
>
> Isaiah 11:2

The throne itself will sit on a beautiful sea of glass that appears to be crystal which represents the magnificence and holiness of God. Surrounding the throne will be four creatures with different faces of animals which are thought to represent God's attributes. The lion represents majesty and power, the (calf) faithfulness, (man) intelligence, and the (eagle) sovereignty. These creatures are not animals, but the highest-ranking angels called Seraphims. They have six wings and are full of eyes. Their job is to guard and praise God continually.

The majesty of his power is portrayed by lightning and thunder and voices projecting out of the throne.

> And out of the throne proceeded lightnings and thunderings and voices:
>
> Revelation 4:5a

There are twenty-four seats with twenty-four elders sitting on them. The exact interpretation is uncertain, but some feel that the twenty-four are made up of twelve patriarchs and twelve apostles from the old and new testaments. Others believe the twenty-four elders are a select group of believers representing the redeemed of all ages. They are dressed in white clothing, representing holiness, and with golden crowns that depict victory and approval from Jesus at His judgment seat.

> And round about the throne were four and twenty seats: and upon the seats I saw four and twenty elders sitting, clothed in white raiment; and they had on their heads crowns of gold.
>
> Revelation 4:4

God's power is further demonstrated at the end of Revelation chapter four when the Seraphims praise, honor, thank and glorify him. At this point the twenty-four will bow before the throne in complete surrender, glorifying and declaring God as their all and all.

> And the four beasts had each of them six wings about him; and they were full of eyes within: and they rest not day and night, saying, Holy, holy, holy, LORD God Almighty, which was, and is, and is to come. ⁹ And when those beasts give glory and honour and thanks to him that sat on the throne, who liveth for ever and ever, The four and twenty elders fall down before him that sat on the throne, and worship him that liveth for ever and ever, and cast their crowns before the throne, saying, 11 Thou art worthy, O Lord, to receive glory and honour and power: for thou hast created all things, and for thy pleasure they are and were created.
>
> Revelation 4:8-11

What a marvelous day for all followers of Christ for we get to participate in this wonderful place called Heaven.

Heaven and End Times

1. Revelation 4:5b, Who do these seven lamps represent?

2. Isaiah 11:2, What are the seven spirits of the Holy Spirit?

3. Revelation 4:4, What is the significance of the elders being dressed in white raiment and the crowns of gold on their heads?

4. Revelation 4:6-9, What are these beasts?

5. Revelation 4:6-9, What is the job of these high-ranking angels called Seraphims?

6. Revelation 4:5, Is lightnings, thunderings, and voices a show of might, judgement, and power?

7. Revelation 4:9-11, Why will the people in white cast their crowns at God's feet?

8. Revelation 5:1, What is in God's right hand?

9. Revelation 5:1, By God holding this book in his right hand does it show that he has the power of when it is to be opened?

10. Revelation 5:2, What does the angel ask?

11. Revelation 5:4, Why did John weep?

12. Revelation 5:5-6, Who is the Lamb that can open the book? Pay strict attention to verse 5.

What does Heaven offer Christians?

What does Heaven offer Christians? This seems like a dumb question, but many do not know the answer. Some do not know how to qualify to go to Heaven let alone what to expect of Heaven. Heaven is not only a place of pure beauty but a haven of love and peace for all who choose Jesus as their savior.

GOD WILL LIVE WITH US:
- Revelation 21:3 And I heard a great voice out of heaven saying, Behold, the tabernacle of God is with men, and he will dwell with them, and they shall be his people, and God himself shall be with them, and be their God.

PROMISE OF TRUE HAPPINESS
- Revelation 21:4 And God shall wipe away all tears from their eyes; and there shall be no more **death**, neither **sorrow**, nor **crying**, neither shall there be any more *pain*: for the former things are passed away.
    - 1). No tears – many things make us cry on earth, but not so in Heaven.
    - 2). No death – no one will die
    - 3). No sorrow – we will no longer feel hurt from the death of loved ones.
    - 4). No pain – our bodies will not experience pain, the broken shall be made whole and pain-free.

WE WILL WORSHIP AND GLORIFY GOD
- Revelation 4:10-11 The four and twenty elders fall down before him that sat on the throne, and **worship him** that liveth for ever and ever, and cast their crowns before the throne, saying, 11 ***Thou art worthy, O Lord, to receive glory and honour and power: for thou hast created all things, and for thy pleasure they are and were created***.
- Revelation 5:13 And every creature which is in heaven, and on the earth, and under the earth, and such as are in the sea, and all that are in them, heard I saying, **Blessing**, and **honour**, and **glory**, and **power**, be unto him that sitteth upon the throne, and unto the Lamb for ever and ever.

NO FINANCIAL WORRIES – No bills! No electricity is needed!
- Revelation 21:23 And the city had no need of the sun, neither of the moon, to shine in it: for the glory of God did lighten it, and the Lamb is the light thereof.

NO SIN
- We know from previous studies that if your name is not found in the Book of Life you will not be allowed in Heaven. The Bible clearly outlines how your name gets in that book and that you will be thrown into the Lake of Fire if your name is not found, therefore no sin is allowed in Heaven.
  - Hebrews 12:14 Follow peace with all men, and **holiness**, *without which no man shall see the Lord:*

SIT WITH JESUS
- Revelation 3:21 To him that overcometh will I grant to sit with me in my throne, even as I also overcame, and am set down with my Father in his throne.

EAT AND DRINK
- Matthew 26:29 But I say unto you, I will not drink henceforth of this fruit of the vine, until that day when I drink it new with you in my Father's kingdom.
- Revelation 19:9 And he saith unto me, Write, Blessed are they which are called unto the marriage supper of the Lamb. And he saith unto me, These are the true sayings of God.

In conclusion, a Christian will be blessed to live in heaven, but how does one achieve Heaven? You must accept Jesus as your savior by acknowledging that Jesus is God's son who died on the cross, was buried and rose again. You must ask for forgiveness and ask Jesus into your heart. I know this sounds too simple, but that is all there is to it.

1. Revelation 21:3, Who will live with us in Heaven?

2. Revelation 21:4, What four things will we no longer experience in Heaven?

3. Revelation 21:23, Will we have electric bills? Why or why not?

4. Revelation 4:10-11, 5:13, What will we do in Heaven?

5. Revelation 5:13, What four things will we give to God?

6. Revelation 21:24, What must you be to enter Heaven?

7. Revelation 21:27, Will there be sin in Heaven?

8. Revelation 3:21, What right will Christians obtain in Heaven?

9. Matthew 26:29, Revelation 19:9, What pleasures are we told we will enjoy?

10. Do you think worshipping God will be burdensome for us? Explain.

What will we do in Heaven?

What will we do in Heaven? Some people are under the misconception that we will just float around in heaven, playing little harps, and have no responsibilities at all. I say we will work and be happy doing it.

Billy Graham also thought as I do, [1]"**God never** intended for people to be idle and unproductive – on earth or in Heaven. Heaven is about serving – not ourselves, but Jesus Christ…" We will create new things, study the world, and do the kinds of work that we love and is pleasing to God. We will never have to worry about hating our jobs in Heaven."

Lesli White, the author of "Will We Work and Have Jobs in Heaven?" said this, [2]"One major difference between work on earth and work in heaven is that we won't grow tired or weary with our work in heaven. *Work became a burden following Adam and Eve's rebellion against God but the minute we enter heaven, the curse is lifted.* We will be delighted in our work there."

> And *there shall be no more curse*: but the throne of God and of the Lamb shall be in it; and *his servants shall serve him*:
> Revelation 22:3

Before this curse, Adam worked but it was enjoyable to work. After the curse, all man's work became hard and strenuous to provide food for themselves and their families. The curse was placed on man after Adam and Eve sinned.

> And unto Adam he said, Because thou hast hearkened unto the voice of thy wife, and hast eaten of the tree, of which I commanded thee, saying, Thou shalt not eat of it: *cursed is the ground for thy sake; in sorrow shalt thou eat of it all the days of thy life;*
> Genesis 3:17

Why should we expect to be any better than God and his son Jesus? They both work, therefore; we should also work.

> But Jesus answered them, *My Father worketh hitherto, and I work.*
> John 5:17

In the parable of the pounds, we see that we will have some sort of authority or work in heaven, be it over others or as workers. Our jobs or positions will be based on our life of servitude to God on earth. Length of salvation does not play into the picture, however; sharing God's word does.

If you have not accepted Jesus as your savior, you will not be rewarded but will find eternal damnation.

Some often wonder why the man that hid his pound in a napkin had his pound taken away and given to the one with ten. The answer is simple, this man was not saved and did not believe that Jesus was the Savior. Again, the saved are rewarded and the unsaved likewise receive their due.

> For I say unto you, That unto every one which hath shall be given; and from him that hath not, even that he hath shall be taken away from him. ^{27} But those **mine enemies, which would not that I should reign over them**, bring hither, and slay them before me.
> Luke 19:26-27

I believe in heaven there will be similar tasks to the current ones performed on earth. I come to this conclusion because of the mention of cities in the parable of the pound. Cities have all kinds of jobs necessary to keep their wheels turning. Jobs from the government to street cleaners. Whatever our job will be, it will not be burdensome, and we will be happy to be in the presence of God and his Son Jesus.

> Come unto me, all ye that labour and are heavy laden, and I will give you rest. ^{29} Take my yoke upon you, and learn of me; for I am meek and lowly in heart: and ye shall find rest unto your souls. ^{30} **For my yoke is easy, and my burden is light**.
> Matthew 11:28-30

> And **there shall be no more curse**: but the throne of God and of the Lamb shall be in it; and **his servants shall serve him**:
> Revelation 22:3

We will also be priests and reign with Jesus in the millennial,

> If we suffer, we shall also **reign with him**: if we deny him, he also will deny us:
> 2 Timothy 2:12

> Blessed and holy is he that hath part in the first resurrection: on such the second death hath no power, but they shall be **priests of God and of Christ, and shall reign with him a thousand years.**
> Revelation 20:6

Our main and most important job will be to glorify God. Some will have the pleasure of being at the foot of his throne and some just by serving in heaven.

> After this I beheld, and, lo, a great multitude, which no man could number, of all nations, and kindreds, and people, and tongues, stood before the throne, and before the Lamb, clothed with white robes, and *palms in their hands.*
>
> Revelation 7:9

> *(The above verse is a reference to Psalm Sunday when palms were placed in front of Jesus, only this time we will truly be worshipping and glorifying God).*

> And I said unto him, Sir, thou knowest. And he said to me, These are they which came out of great Tribulation, and have washed their robes, and made them white in the blood of the Lamb. *15 Therefore are they before the throne of God, and serve him day and night in his temple: and he that sitteth on the throne shall dwell among them.*
>
> Revelation 7:14-15

I am glad we will have jobs in heaven. I speak from the experience of being retired. For years I looked forward to not having to work every day but upon retirement found that I cannot sit and not do anything. One of the perks of being retired is I can do things when I want or take off and enjoy local beauty with my husband. I believe Heaven will be like this. I cannot imagine an eternity of not doing anything and being bored. I believe there will be work, an abundance of love, fun, and beauty for all. Most of all we will find our greatest pleasure will be glorifying God.

---

[1] Will there be Work and Cultures in Heaven? (christianworldviewpress.com), Will there be Work and Cultures in Heaven? Category: The End Times, Theology July 1, 2014, Billy Graham. The *Heaven Answer Book* (Nashville: Thomas Nelson, 2012). 49.

[2] Will We Work and Have Jobs in Heaven? - Beliefnet, Will We Work and Have Jobs in Heaven?, Leslie White, as of December 8, 2021

1. Genesis 3:17, When did work become a curse?

2. Revelation 22:3, Matthew 11:28-30, What will we do in Heaven, and will it be considered hard?

3. John 5:17, Why do you think we are expected to work on earth?

4. If God works and He is in Heaven, do you think we will also work when we go to Heaven?

5. Luke 19:16-19, These men will be given authority over cities. What must one do to have authority?

6. Luke 19:20-27, Was this man saved?

7. 2 Timothy 2:12, What will Jesus do if we deny him?

8. 2 Timothy 2:12, Revelation 20:6, What jobs will the saved have in the millennial?

9. John 12:13, What were these people doing?

10. Luke 19:11, What did the people think should immediately appear?

11. Mark 15:13, When thee people saw that Jesus was not there to physically save them. Within days of worshipping him with palms, what do they want to do?

12. Revelation 7:9, 7:14-15, What will be our most important job?

Our Mansion in Heaven

We have all heard that we will have a mansion in heaven and automatically our minds envision the big, beautiful mansions of movie stars. This vision not only stems from our physical sight here on earth but also the biblical description of Heaven.

As we studied earlier, Heaven has walls made of beautiful gems, giant pearl gates, streets of clear gold, and a crystal river running from God's Throne. The Throne itself is a masterpiece of beauty with its Jasper and Sardine stones surrounded by an emerald rainbow with seven magnificent lamps of fire placed in front of it.

Jesus himself told us we will have a mansion,

> In my Father's house are many **mansions**: if it were not so, I would have told you. I go to prepare a place for you. ³And if I go and prepare a place for you, I will come again, and receive you unto myself; that where I am, there ye may be also.
>
> John 14:2-3

So now one cheers, YES! Jesus said we will have a real mansion! But let us not get too excited. In the days of Jesus, a mansion according to the KJV Dictionary meant: *"Any place of residence; a house; a habitation. In this verse the Greek definition is Abode which Merriam-Webster Dictionary states means, the place where one lives;* ***home****.*" I do not know about you but, I cannot think of a better home.

The Middle Eastern culture during Jesus' time often added many rooms onto their home to accommodate extended family members. Jesus could have been painting a picture that one would be considered as an extended family member and have a room. If you think about it as a Christian, you are a legal heir of God and co-heir with Christ and therefore an extended family member.

> And if children, then heirs; heirs of God, and joint heirs with Christ; if so be that we suffer with him, that we may be also glorified together.
>
> Romans 8:17

Another theory is that our home will be just a standing spot in heaven with all the saved people of the world, in the presence of God.

> After this I beheld, and, lo, a great multitude, which no man could number, of all nations, and kindreds, and people, and tongues, **_stood before the throne, and before the Lamb_**, clothed with white robes, and palms in their hands;
> Revelation 7:9

Adam and Eve were created by God and placed in a perfect world. They never had to worry if it would be too hot, dry, wet, windy, or cold because of the canopy that surrounded the earth. The animals all lived peacefully together. Adam and Eve's only job was to care for God's creation. Nothing is mentioned about where they lived, but it mattered not because it was perfect.

It will not matter to us either if we have a mansion, a hut, a room, or just a standing place because all things are perfect and beautiful in Heaven, and we will be in the presence of God. However, I believe we will at least have a room or Jesus would not have made a point to tell us he is preparing one for us.

Heaven and End Times

1. John 14:2-3, Are we guaranteed a mansion in Heaven? Explain.

2. Does the word mansion have other meanings besides a large elaborate home? What are some of them?

3. Do you think it will matter to us if our mansion is just a small room or standing spot to worship God?

4. 1 Timothy 5:8, Is talking about providing for family members (widows, etc.) that are in dire need. During this time families were expected to care for them. Do you think housing provisions would be customary?

5. Romans 8:17, Are we considered God's children?

6. Revelation 7:9, and Revelation 21:25, Some believe we will only have a standing spot? Do you believe this to be true? Explain.

7. 1 Corinthians 2:9, Do you think that God will provide for us a place to stay?

8. Revelation 21:24-26, Do you believe we will come within the gates to worship God but many will live outside the walls, as the gates are never shut?

9. Revelation 14:13, We are told we will work in Heaven, but here we are told we will also rest. Do you think this means we will indeed have a place to rest?

Will there be Time in Heaven?

When we think of time, we think of the hurried fast-paced world we live in today. Will Heaven be the same? I believe not.

The Bible describes Heaven in great detail, but very little is said about time. Some believe that there will be no time, and some believe there will be time. We will look at both scenarios.

The Bible does tell us there will not be a sun or a moon. This is the argument used to support the theory that there will be no time. But remember we are talking Heaven. Earth's time is measured by the sun and the moon, not necessarily Heaven's.

> And the city had no need of the sun, neither of the moon, to shine in it: for the glory of God did lighten it, and the Lamb is the light thereof.
>
> Revelation 21:23

One reason I believe there will be time is that God's word tells us that there will be months.

> And he shewed me a pure river of water of life, clear as crystal, proceeding out of the throne of God and of the Lamb. ² In the midst of the street of it, and on either side of the river, was there the tree of life, which bare twelve manner of fruits, and yielded her fruit ***every month***: and the leaves of the tree were for the healing of the nations.
>
> Revelation 22:1-2

Peter hinted to us that there is time in heaven (God's time), but it is vastly different than our time.

> But, beloved, be not ignorant of this one thing, that one day is with the Lord as a thousand years, and a thousand years as one day.
>
> 2 Peter 3:8

John said in Revelation that there was silence in Heaven for a half hour,

> And when he had opened the seventh seal, there was silence in heaven about the space of ***half an hour***.
>
> Revelation 8:1

These most ensuring words point to a measurement of time,

> Verily, verily, I say unto you, He that heareth my word, and believeth on him that sent me, hath ***everlasting life***, and shall not come into condemnation; but is passed from death unto life.
>
> John 5:24

So, what does the word everlasting mean? When applying to God, it means without beginning or end. When applying to man it means; has a beginning but no end. In a nutshell, Christians will live with God in heaven FOREVER! I hope this happy news gets an amen from all of you.

In conclusion, it does not matter if there is time in Heaven or not. We will be with God forever and that is the only time that matters.

Deborah L. Gladwell

1. Revelation 21:23, What is missing in Heaven that we measure time by on earth?

2. James 4:14, How does the Bible describe the length of our life on earth?

3. John 5:24, In the above question we saw that our life on earth is like a vapor and quickly vanishes. How long will our life be in Heaven according to John?

4. 2 Peter 3:8, Peter compared one day of our time to God's time. How long did he say a day would be in God's time?

5. Revelation 22:1-2, What component of time is mentioned here?

6. Revelation 8:1, What component of time is mentioned here?

7. Hebrews 13:8, Jesus will be the same _____?

8. Revelation 6:9-10, The martyred are asking how _____ before they are revenged. Is that a component of time?

9. Revelation 22:5, How long will God's servants reign with Him and Jesus?

Purgatory?

What is purgatory? Is it biblical? We will study how the belief in Purgatory came about and if it is biblical. The best description of purgatory I found was given by author Hope Bolinger, [1]*"Purgatory is believed by some as a place for sinners who have God's grace but need to endure "temporal punishment" for transgressions that did not receive payment during their lives. In other words, if anyone has any leftover sin, this place purges them of it, before they reach the gates of heaven."* A place of torture to repent from one's sins.

The catholic church believes you can pray people out of purgatory. Is this possible? I believe not, but we will study.

[2]*"The Prayer of St. Gertrude, below, is one of the most famous of the prayers for souls in purgatory. St. Gertrude the Great was a Benedictine nun and mystic who lived in the 13th century. According to tradition, our Lord promised her that 1000 souls would be released from purgatory each time it is said devoutly. Whether or not this is actually the case, this is a great prayer for focusing on helping the Holy Souls in Purgatory nonetheless:* **Eternal Father, I offer Thee the Most Precious Blood of Thy Divine Son, Jesus, in union with the masses said throughout the world today, for all the holy souls in purgatory, for sinners everywhere, for sinners in the universal church, those in my own home and within my family. Amen."**

The theory that you can pray someone out of purgatory is based on a book found in the Apocrypha. [3]*"2 Maccabees 12:46 It is therefore a holy and wholesome thought to pray for the dead, that they may be loosed from sins."*

The Apocrypha is not considered to be part of the Bible because it is not inspired by God, but it does contain some historical facts

[4,5]Matthias Maccabean a priest, sparked the Maccabean Revolt by refusing to worship and sacrifice to idols. After his death, his son Judas Maccabean led the Maccabean Revolt against the Seleucid Empire (167–160 BCE). The Jewish festival of Hanukkah celebrates the re-dedication of the Temple following Judah Maccabee's victory over the Seleucids.

It is also customary to take up a memorial Mass for the dead. This Mass is for the benefit of someone in purgatory. It is a custom to give the parish priest a stipend. If you notice this custom appears to be based on "2 Maccabbe 12:43 *And making a gathering, he sent twelve thousand drachms of silver to Jerusalem for sacrifice to be offered for the sins of the dead, thinking well and religiously concerning the resurrection,*

Let us look at the full picture of Purgatory and why many believe you can pray or buy people's way out of it as given by Maccabee. [2] "*2 Maccabee 12:39-46 And the day following Judas came with his company, to take away the bodies of them that were slain, and to bury them with their kinsmen, in the sepulchres of their fathers.* **⁴⁰ And they found under the coats of the slain some of the donaries of the idols of Jamnia, which the law forbiddeth to the Jews: so that all plainly saw, that for this cause they were slain**. *⁴¹ Then they all blessed the just judgment of the Lord, who had discovered the things that were hidden. ⁴² And so betaking themselves to prayers, they besought him, that the sin which had been committed might be forgotten. But the most valiant Judas exhorted the people to keep themselves from sin, forasmuch as they saw before their eyes what had happened, because of the sins of those that were slain.* **⁴³ And making a gathering, he sent twelve thousand drachms of silver to Jerusalem for sacrifice to be offered for the sins of the dead, thinking well and religiously concerning the resurrection,** *⁴⁴ (For if he had not hoped that they that were slain should rise again, it would have seemed superfluous and vain to pray for the dead,) ⁴⁵ And because he considered that they who had fallen asleep with godliness, had great grace laid up for them.* **⁴⁶ It is therefore a holy and wholesome thought to pray for the dead, that they may be loosed from sins.**"

I have a few problems with this teaching:
- The book of 2 Maccabee is not found in our Bible. We are clearly ordered not to add to or subtract from God's Holy Word, which is our Bible.
  - <u>Deuteronomy 4:2</u> Ye shall not add unto the word which I command you, neither shall ye diminish ought from it, that ye may keep the commandments of the Lord your God which I command you.
  - <u>Revelation 22:18</u> For I testify unto every man that heareth the words of the prophecy of this book, If any man shall add unto these things, God shall add unto him the plagues that are written in this book:
- The whole revolt was to end sacrificing to idols. Please note in verse 40, that on the persons of the dead were found idolatry items.
- If one believes that they can be prayed by others to Heaven after death or have their way paid to Heaven after death. Then they do not believe that Jesus paid it all on the cross.

Let's look at some Bible verses that others use to back the rituals of Purgatory, along with why they are being misinterpreted:

The following verse is referring to refining people on earth, not Heaven.

> When the Lord shall have washed away the filth of the daughters of Zion, and shall have purged the blood of Jerusalem from the midst thereof by the spirit of judgment, and by the spirit of burning.
> Isaiah 4:4

Jesus was teaching us to settle our differences before it reaches the judge (not God).

> Agree with thine adversary quickly, whiles thou art in the way with him; lest at any time the adversary **deliver thee to the judge**, and **the judge deliver thee to the officer, and thou be cast into prison**.26 Verily I say unto thee, Thou shalt by no means come out thence, till thou hast paid the uttermost farthing.
> Matthew 5:25-26

Confusion arises from the wording of this world or the world to come. It merely means *Never*! Mark 3:29 and Luke 12:10 relate to the same message but more precise wording. Folks never means Never!

> And whosoever speaketh a word against the Son of man, it shall be forgiven him: but whosoever speaketh against the Holy Ghost, it shall not be forgiven him, **neither in this world, neither in the world to come**.
> Matthew 12:32

Hebrews is not referring to a judgement and then you pay a price and go to heaven.

> And as it is appointed unto men once to die, but after this the judgment:
> Hebrews 9:27

In conclusion, we go directly to Jesus after death. We have no opportunity to repent after we die. Those who believe in Jesus as their savior are already justified by his shed blood. Jesus paid it all for us.

> We are confident, I say, and willing rather to be absent from the body, and to be present with the Lord.
> 2 Corinthians 5:8

And by him all that believe are justified from all things, from which ye could not be justified by the law of Moses.

Acts 13:39

Verily, verily, I say unto you, He that heareth my word, and believeth on him that sent me, hath everlasting life, and shall not come into condemnation; but is passed from death unto life.

John 5:24

References

[1] What Is Purgatory? Definition and Biblical Doctrine Explained (christianity.com), Hope Bolinger, August 21, 2020

[2] https://www.ourcatholicprayers.com/prayers-for-souls-in-purgatory.html , Our Catholic Prayers, As of December 8, 2021

[3] 1 Maccabees 2 KJV (apocrypha.org)

[4,5] Maccabean Revolt - Wikipedia , Judas Maccabeus - Wikipedia , From Wikipedia, the free encyclopedia, as of December 8, 2021

Heaven and End Times

1. What is Purgatory?

2. Why is the Apocrypha not considered to be part of the Bible?

3. Is the Apocrypha a source for historical information?

4. 2 Maccabee 12:43, Talks of a money sacrifice for the sins of the dead. Read John 14:6, Ephesians 2:8-9 Can you pay someone's way to Heaven? Explain.

5. 1 Corinthians 10:20-21, What does God say about idol worshipping?

6. Exodus 20:3-6, God does not approve of idol worshipping. He says he is what kind of God?

7. Judges 10:14, Who does God tell idol worshipers to go to when they are in trouble?

8. Do you believe people who worship idols are truly saved?

9. According to 2 Maccabee 12:39-46, the dead had items of the idol of Jamnia. A monetary sacrifice was offered for their sins. Verse 46 states that it is "holy and wholesome thought to pray for the dead, that they may be loosed from sins."
   - John 5:24 tells us that those who have accepted Jesus as their saviour pass from death unto life. No in-between is mentioned.
   - 2 Corinthians 5:8, tells us to be absent from the body is to be present with the Lord. No in-between was mentioned.

So, according to the Bible is there a Purgatory?

10. Luke 16:24-26, If you die unsaved can you cross from Hell to Heaven?

11. Deuteronomy 4:2, Revelation 22:18, Are we to accept anything taught that is not found in our Bible?

12. Acts 13:39, Do you believe Christians will have to pay a price or spend time in Purgatory, or are we already justified?

Is Coronavirus the beginning of the End Times?

The coronavirus which started in 2019, has some people fearful of reopening America and labeling people greedy. Meanwhile, more suicides happened in two weeks than in a normal one-year period, terminally ill patients were not getting medical procedures, the elderly died alone in nursing homes, and working people continued to lose their means to support their families.

If we stay shut down and the Government quits printing worthless money, as it did during the Great Depression. There will not be any welfare or financial aid of any kind! So, those who are Government dependent will also lose their livelihoods.

MOST of today's society has never experienced extreme poverty without anyone to bail them out. Some of the older generations have experienced very TIGHT times but still not like a Depression. Some of us have had to take hand-me-down clothes, shoes, etc., and were thrilled to receive them. We listened to our Parents and Grandparents regarding how bad the Depression was. We learned to conserve and to make life easier for our children, however; we have gone too far with handouts. Handouts were meant to be a temporary hand up not a lifestyle.

We now have people who think it is criminal to want to support our families. They see nothing wrong with a socialist type of society that is completely dependent on the Government. Mayors are asking people to snitch on others as did Hitler. People we cannot hide in our homes forever while politicians play their fear mind controlling games. That is not living, it is a voluntary death sentence.

This holing up concept is even used to suppress our religious freedoms. It is finely orchestrated by Satan himself. Think about it, people can go to Walmart, the beach, bars but in some states, one cannot lawfully hold church. Come on people open your eyes before it is too late.

We are hearing phrases such as, "The New Norm". Are we going to be a mask-wearing, non-touching non-compassionate human race? Is this the norm you want? Not me! A touch or smile is what makes us feel for others, do away with them and any feeling we have left as human beings will start to disappear. Use commonsense but let us not let fear control us!

> Fear thou not; for I am with thee: be not dismayed; for I am thy God: I will strengthen thee; yea, I will help thee; yea, I will uphold thee with the right hand of my righteousness.
>
> Isaiah 41:10

Jesus tells us that the closer we get to the end of times we will see more pestilence (diseases)

> And great earthquakes shall be in divers places, and famines, and ***pestilences***; and fearful sights and great signs shall there be from heaven.
>
> Luke 21:11

> For nation shall rise against nation, and kingdom against kingdom: and there shall be famines, and ***pestilences***, and earthquakes, in divers places.
>
> Matthew 24:7

So, is the coronavirus the beginning of the end? I do not know because the Bible tells us no man knows. Either way, I believe current events point toward one big wake-up call for our world. We all better know Jesus as our Savior and be grounded in his word (the Bible) for hard times could be just around the corner.

> Watch therefore, for ye know neither the day nor the hour wherein the Son of man cometh.
>
> Matthew 25:13

Will we be raptured to Jesus or will we be found in the Tribulation? I hope with all my heart we will be found with Jesus. Please make sure this will be your case.

Deborah L. Gladwell

1. 1 Timothy 5:8, Tells us if we do not work to support our families, we are worse than an _____?

2. 1 Timothy 6:6-8, In verse 8 what should we be content if we have?

3. Hebrews 10:25, Romans 10:17, and 1 Corinthians 16:13, Should we forsake assembling?

4. 1 Peter 5:8, What is happening here?

5. Acts 8:3, 9:1-2, We are told history repeats itself. Could this newfound power the Government has over us due to COVID regulations lead to the same persecution?

6. 1 John 2:15-17, James 4:4, Satan wants us to believe that we can participate in worldly ways and still go to Heaven, can we?

7. Isaiah 41:10, Who will help us stay strong?

8. Luke 21:11, Matthew 24:7, Will there be many diseases closer to the end of time?

9. Matthew 25:13, Does anyone know when the end of time will take place?

The Red Heifer!

Why must the red heifer have no spots and be blemish-free? What in the world can a red heifer have to do with end times? Have two temples been built? What happened to them? Will there be a third Temple of God? If all it takes is a red heifer for the Third Temple to be built, why has it not been built? Are these things biblical and how do they relate to Christians and Jews? Let us see if we can find the answers.

In the Old Testament God directly instructed Moses how to purify the tabernacle of the congregation. Please note his instructions were for a red heifer without spot or blemish and never had been yoked.

> This is the ordinance of the law which the Lord hath commanded, saying, Speak unto the children of Israel, that they ***bring thee a red heifer without spot, wherein is no blemish***, ***and upon which never came yoke:*** 3 And ye shall give her unto Eleazar the priest, that he may bring her forth without the camp, and one shall slay her before his face: 4 And Eleazar the priest shall take of her blood with his finger, and sprinkle of her blood directly before the tabernacle of the congregation seven times: 5 And one shall burn the heifer in his sight; her skin, and her flesh, and her blood, with her dung, shall he burn: 6 And the priest shall take cedar wood, and hyssop, and scarlet, and cast it into the midst of the burning of the heifer. 7 Then the priest shall wash his clothes, and he shall bathe his flesh in water, and afterward he shall come into the camp, and the priest shall be unclean until the even.
>
> Numbers 19:2-7

King Solomon built the first temple of God. We are given the exact measurements, material, etc. in 1 Kings 6. But how do we know this temple was built by Solomon?

> And he said unto me, Solomon thy son, he shall build my house and my courts: for I have chosen him to be my son, and I will be his father.
>
> 1 Chronicles 28:6

> And the word of the LORD came to Solomon, saying, [12] Concerning this house which thou art in building, if thou wilt walk in my statutes, and execute my judgments, and keep all my commandments to walk in them; then will I perform my word with thee, which I spake unto David thy father: [13] And I will dwell among

the children of Israel, and will not forsake my people Israel. ¹⁴ So Solomon built the house, and finished it.

1 Kings 6:11-14

What happened to the first Temple? It was destroyed by Babylon:

> And in the fifth month, on the seventh day of the month, which is the nineteenth year of king Nebuchadnezzar king of Babylon, came Nebuzaradan, captain of the guard, a servant of the king of Babylon, unto Jerusalem: ⁹ And he burnt the house of the LORD, and the king's house, and all the houses of Jerusalem, and every great man's house burnt he with fire. ¹⁰ And all the army of the Chaldees, that were with the captain of the guard, brake down the walls of Jerusalem round about. ¹¹ Now the rest of the people that were left in the city, and the fugitives that fell away to the king of Babylon, with the remnant of the multitude, did Nebuzaradan the captain of the guard carry away. ¹² But the captain of the guard left of the poor of the land to be vinedressers and husbandmen. ¹³ And the pillars of brass that were in the house of the LORD, and the bases, and the brasen sea that was in the house of the LORD, did the Chaldees break in pieces, and carried the brass of them to Babylon. ¹⁴ And the pots, and the shovels, and the snuffers, and the spoons, and all the vessels of brass wherewith they ministered, took they away. ¹⁵ And the firepans, and the bowls, and such things as were of gold, in gold, and of silver, in silver, the captain of the guard took away.

2 Kings 25:8-15

The building of the second temple took place over a longer period of time. God used two nonchristian kings to start the rebuilding process. King Cyrus the king of Babylon and King Darius both made decrees to not only build the temple but also gave instructions on how to rebuild. They even gave back everything Babylon took from the first temple. Zerubbabel (who the second temple is dedicated to), Joshua son of Josedech, the high priest of the time, and a remnant of God's people, built the temple.

> Then Darius the king made a decree, and search was made in the house of the rolls, where the treasures were laid up in Babylon. ² And there was found at Achmetha, in the palace that is in the province of the Medes, a roll, and therein was a record thus written: ³In the first year of Cyrus the king the same Cyrus the king made a decree concerning the house of God at Jerusalem, Let the house be builded, the place where they offered sacrifices, and let the foundations thereof be strongly laid; the height thereof threescore cubits, and the breadth thereof threescore cubits; ⁴ With three rows

of great stones, and a row of new timber: and let the expenses be given out of the king's house: ⁵ And also let the golden and silver vessels of the house of God, which Nebuchadnezzar took forth out of the temple which is at Jerusalem, and brought unto Babylon, be restored, and brought again unto the temple which is at Jerusalem, every one to his place, and place them in the house of God.

Ezra 6:1-5

In the second year of Darius the king, in the sixth month, in the first day of the month, came the word of the LORD by Haggai the prophet unto Zerubbabel the son of Shealtiel, governor of Judah, and to Joshua the son of Josedech, the high priest, saying, ² Thus speaketh the LORD of hosts, saying, This people say, The time is not come, the time that the LORD's house should be built. ³ Then came the word of the LORD by Haggai the prophet, saying, ⁴ Is it time for you, O ye, to dwell in your cieled houses, and this house lie waste? ⁵ Now therefore thus saith the LORD of hosts; Consider your ways… ¹⁴And the Lord stirred up the spirit of Zerubbabel the son of Shealtiel, governor of Judah, and the spirit of Joshua the son of Josedech, the high priest, and the spirit of all the remnant of the people; and they came and did work in the house of the Lord of hosts, their God,

Haggai 1:1-5,14

Jesus warned the second temple would fall because people were not honoring God in it. The veil of the temple was torn from top to bottom upon his death:

And Jesus went into the temple of God, and cast out all them that sold and bought in the temple, and overthrew the tables of the moneychangers, and the seats of them that sold doves, ¹³ And said unto them, It is written, My house shall be called the house of prayer; but ye have made it a den of thieves.

Matthew 21:12-13

And Jesus went out, and departed from the temple: and his disciples came to him for to shew him the buildings of the temple. ² And Jesus said unto them, See ye not all these things? verily I say unto you, There shall not be left here one stone upon another, that shall not be thrown down.

Matthew 24:1-2

And Jesus cried with a loud voice, and gave up the ghost. ³⁸ And the veil of the temple was rent in twain from the top to the bottom.

Mark 15:37-38

Today's rabbis believe that all materials necessary to rebuild the third temple are unclean. They must purify the Temple mount according to God's instructions using a perfect Red Heifer. They will not build God's Temple until everything involved with the temple is properly cleansed.

The answer to the question, "Will there be a third Temple of God?", is yes. Prophecy is already starting to unfold which means the rapture might be soon. Although we are not told exactly when it will be built, many believe it will happen right before the Tribulation. We do know the Antichrist will declare he is God during the Tribulation and take residence in it. We also know that Paul was told to measure the Temple.

> Let no man deceive you by any means: for that day shall not come, except there come a falling away first, and that man of sin be revealed, the son of perdition; 4 Who opposeth and exalteth himself above all that is called God, or that is worshipped; s*o that he as God sitteth in the temple of God, shewing himself that he is God*.
>
> 2 Thessalonians 2:3-4

> And there was given me a reed like unto a rod: and the angel stood, saying, **Rise, and measure the temple of God**, and the altar, and them that worship therein. 2 But the court which is without the temple leave out, and measure it not; for it is given unto the Gentiles: and the holy city shall they tread under foot forty and two months. 3 And I will give power unto my two witnesses, and they shall prophesy a thousand two hundred and threescore days, clothed in sackcloth.
>
> Revelation 11:1-3

Why has there not been a red heifer to fulfill this prophecy in 2,000 years? There are many reasons. One major reason is that Israel itself was only reestablished in 1948. Then there is the requirement that it must be a red heifer (female) which decreases the odds, plus it must be spot-free and have no blemishes which further shrinks the odds. Also, this heifer must be born from a natural birth, have no more than two non-red hairs on its body, never have been used for any labor, be two years old, and never have been impregnated. Furthermore, we must consider that all things follow God's timetable.

Where did the other requirements come from, such as the age of the heifer, that it must be from a natural birth, and never have been impregnated? The answer is pretty simple, it is the Jewish Law, and they are the ones that will not only build the temple but also provide the heifer to cleanse the mound.

It is my understanding there are at least four candidates to fulfill the necessary qualifications but remember it must be at least two years old, and it will be hard in that time span not to acquire some kind of blemish.

Christians do not believe we need a sacrifice as Jesus was the ultimate sacrifice, however; it is the Jewish belief that there must be a Red Heifer sacrifice and cleansing before the temple can be built. According to the Bible, it must be the Jewish people who rebuild God's Temple. Christians believe Jesus has already come and will return in the End Times. The Jewish believe he is yet to come. Either way, the Temple is important to both faiths. Although our beliefs are different, the Temple will not be built until God's complete plan is in place. All these things are found in the Bible.

1. 1 Chronicles 28:6, Who built the first temple?

2. 2 Kings 25:8-9, Who destroyed the first temple?

3. 2 Kings 25:13-15, What was taken from the first temple?

4. Ezra 6:3-5, King Cyrus and King Darius gave what back to build the second temple?

5. Mark 15:38 and Matthew 21:12-13, Why do you think the veil of the second temple was torn in two upon Jesus' death?

6. Numbers 19:2, What does Moses say God gave him?

7. Numbers 19:2, Is this something they can choose to do or not do? Explain.

8. Numbers 19:2, What qualities must the red heifer have?

9. Why do you think God requires the red heifer to be perfect?

10. Numbers 19:4-7, Why do you think the Priest was considered unclean after he completed the cleansing?

Can You Get Saved After the Rapture?

Some say that after Jesus raptures Christians, no one can get saved. They are greatly confused because as long as one breathes, they have the chance of getting right with God. They deduce that the Tribulation will be God's punishment for the unsaved. Although it is true about the punishment of the unsaved, there will still be those who choose Salvation during this horrific time. As I stated before they will be saved but they are going to suffer along with the unsaved.

The Bible tells us during the Tribulation, that 144,000 people of the Jewish faith will be sealed by God and will later be saved. These 144,000 will receive God's seal on their forehead marking them as his servants. It is my opinion this could represent the same purpose as the blood above the doorpost at Passover.

> And I heard the number of them which were sealed: and there were sealed an hundred and forty and four thousand of all the tribes of the children of Israel.
>
> Revelation 7:4

The 144,000 will accept Jesus as their savior. Please note, *"the Lamb"* is Jesus Christ. The Bible states that they are found redeemed with no-fault and are firstfruits unto God and the Lamb.

> These are they which were not defiled with women; for they are virgins. These are they which follow **the Lamb** whithersoever he goeth. These were redeemed from among men, being the firstfruits unto God and to **the Lamb**. 5 And in their mouth was found no guile: for they are without fault before the throne of God.
>
> Revelation 14:4-5

The final chance to repent will be just before the end of the Tribulation. God will send an angel to preach the gospel *(good news)*. Never in the history of man have angels preached to mankind. This is an indication of how much evil will be present on earth.

> And I saw another angel fly in the midst of heaven, having the everlasting gospel to preach unto them that dwell on the earth, and to every nation, and kindred, and tongue, and people, 7 Saying with a loud voice, Fear God, and give glory to him; for the hour of his judgment is come: and worship him that made heaven, and earth, and the sea, and the fountains of waters.
>
> Revelation 14:6-7

We saw that 144,000 Jewish people were sealed, saved, and protected from the destruction that was coming. But does that mean only Jewish people will be saved during the Tribulation? No, if you recall, there will be two prophets and later an angel will preach salvation to **the whole earth**. Also, remember the Antichrist and False Prophet will require people to take on the Mark of the Beast to buy or sell goods. Those who choose not to receive this mark will be tortured or killed. The Beast (Antichrist) and False Prophet will reign during the Tribulation. I, therefore, conclude these people will be saved during the Tribulation.

> And I saw thrones, and they sat upon them, and judgment was given unto them: *and I saw the souls of them that were beheaded for the witness of Jesus, and for the word of God, and which had not worshipped the beast, neither his image, neither had received his mark upon their foreheads, or in their hands;* and they lived and reigned with Christ a thousand years.
> Revelation 20:4

> And I will give power unto *my two witnesses*, and they shall prophesy a thousand two hundred and threescore days, clothed in sackcloth.
> Revelation 11:3

> And I saw another *angel* fly in the midst of heaven, having the everlasting gospel *to preach unto them that dwell on the earth, and to every nation, and kindred, and tongue, and people*, ⁷Saying with a loud voice, Fear God, and give glory to him; for the hour of his judgment is come: and worship him that made heaven, and earth, and the sea, and the fountains of waters.
> Revelation 14:6-7

I believe that some will flee to remote areas and will escape receiving the mark of the Beast. They will either accept Jesus as their Saviour on their own or perhaps by the two witnesses or maybe even by the angel. I believe this because during the seventh seal the prayers of saints are heard. Also, the saved are harvested in a later chapter to a safe place.

> And the smoke of the incense, which came with the prayers of the saints, ascended up before God out of the angel's hand.
> Revelation 8:4

> And I looked, and behold a white cloud, and upon the cloud one sat like unto the Son of man, having on his head a golden crown, and

in his hand a sharp sickle. ¹⁵ And another angel came out of the temple, crying with a loud voice to him that sat on the cloud, Thrust in thy sickle, and reap: for the time is come for thee to reap; for the harvest of the earth is ripe. ¹⁶ And he that sat on the cloud thrust in his sickle on the earth; and the earth was reaped.
Revelation 14:14-16

Immediately after the tribulation of those days shall the sun be darkened, and the moon shall not give her light, and the stars shall fall from heaven, and the powers of the heavens shall be shaken: ³⁰ And then shall appear the sign of the Son of man in heaven: and then shall all the tribes of the earth mourn, and they shall see the Son of man coming in the clouds of heaven with power and great glory. ³¹ And he shall send his angels with a great sound of a trumpet, and they shall gather together his elect from the four winds, from one end of heaven to the other.
Matthew 24:29-31

The Bible states there will be Christians saved after the Tribulation begins:

And I said unto him, Sir, thou knowest. And he said to me, ***These are they which came out of great Tribulation,*** and have washed their robes, and made them white in the blood of the Lamb.
Revelation 7:14

The martyred in Heaven are told to wait for their brethren (fellow Christians) to join them. This will take place during the Tribulation.

And white robes were given unto every one of them; and it was said unto them, that they should rest yet for a little season, until their fellowservants also and their brethren, that should be killed as they were, should be fulfilled.
Revelation 6:11

Finally, remember the plan of Salvation itself only requires you to believe that Jesus is God's Son and for you to call upon him to be your Saviour.

And brought them out, and said, Sirs, what must I do to be saved? ³¹ And they said, Believe on the Lord Jesus Christ, and thou shalt be saved, and thy house.
Acts 16:30-31

For whosoever shall call upon the name of the Lord shall be saved.
Romans 10:13

1. Revelation 7:4, How many Jews will be sealed in the Tribulation?

2. Revelation 7:4-8, The 144,000 sealed Jews are from the tribes of Israel. What are the names of these tribes?

3. Revelation 14:4, Who is the Lamb?

4. Revelation 14:4, What do you think, "These were redeemed from among men, being the firstfruits unto God, and to the Lamb." Means?

5. Revelation 11:3-7, and Revelation 14:6-7, Will the message of Salvation still be preached? If yes by who?

6. Revelation 13:14-18, What would happen to anyone who did not take the mark of the Beast?

7. Revelation 14:14-16, Matthew 24:29-31, Do these verses indicate that are people that were saved during the Tribulation?

8. Revelation 20:4, and Revelation 7:14, Do you believe these were saved people from the time of the Tribulation? Explain.

9. Revelation 6:11, What are the martyred told by God?

10. Romans 10:13, and Acts 16:30-31, The plan of Salvation just requires what?

11. According to question number 10, Do you believe people will get saved during the Tribulation?

Will Christians go through the Tribulation?

What is the Tribulation, and will Christians go through it? The Tribulation is a seven-year period in which God will discipline Israel and release his wrath on unbelievers.

> Behold, the day of the LORD cometh, cruel both with wrath and fierce anger, to lay the land desolate: and he shall destroy the sinners thereof out of it.
>
> Isaiah 13:9

According to Bible prophecy, the Tribulation will occur during what we call, "the End Times".

> For in those days shall be affliction, such as was not from the beginning of the creation which God created unto this time, neither shall be.
>
> Mark 13:19

The Bible gives us many clues about the End Times, some have already come true.

> This know also, that *in the last days* perilous times shall come. 2 For men shall be lovers of their own selves, covetous, boasters, proud, blasphemers, disobedient to parents, unthankful, unholy, 3 Without natural affection, trucebreakers, false accusers, incontinent, fierce, despisers of those that are good, 4 Traitors, heady, highminded, lovers of pleasures more than lovers of God; 5 Having a form of godliness, but denying the power thereof: from such turn away. 6 For of this sort are they which creep into houses, and lead captive silly women laden with sins, led away with divers lusts, 7 Ever learning, and never able to come to the knowledge of the truth.
>
> 2 Timothy 3:1 7

> And ye shall hear of wars and rumors of wars: see that ye be not troubled: for all these things must come to pass, but the end is not yet.
>
> Matthew 24:6

> And great earthquakes shall be in divers places, and famines, and pestilences; and fearful sights and great signs shall there be from heaven.
>
> Luke 21:11

What does Rapture mean, and will the raptured Christians endure the Tribulation? Rapture means that those who are saved by the shed blood of Jesus Christ will be taken from the earth **_before_** the Tribulation period and thankfully will not experience God's wrath.

> But as the days of Noah were, so shall also the coming of the Son of man be. 38 For as in the days that were before the flood they were eating and drinking, marrying and giving in marriage, until the day that Noe entered into the ark, 39 And knew not until the flood came, and took them all away; *so shall also the coming of the Son of man be. 40 Then shall two be in the field; the one shall be taken, and the other left. 41 Two women shall be grinding at the mill; the one shall be taken, and the other left. 42 Watch therefore: for ye know not what hour your Lord doth come.*
>
> Matthew 24:37-42

> And at that time shall Michael stand up, the great prince which standeth for the children of thy people: and there shall be a time of trouble, such as never was since there was a nation even to that same time: *and at that time thy people shall be delivered, every one that shall be found written in the book.*
>
> Daniel 12:1

> For the Lord himself shall descend from heaven with a shout, with the voice of the archangel, and with the trump of God: and the dead in Christ shall rise first: *17 Then we which are alive and remain shall be caught up together with them in the clouds, to meet the Lord in the air: and so shall we ever be with the Lord.*
>
> 1 Thessalonians 4:16-17

All people saved after the rapture will have to experience the Tribulation and many will be tortured. Please note that saint(s) is the term used in the Bible for Christians. We are told that the Beast (Antichrist) will make war with the saints.

> And it was given unto him to make war with the **_saints_**, and to overcome them: and power was given him over all kindreds, and tongues, and nations. 8 And all that dwell upon the earth shall worship him, whose names are not written in the book of life of the

Heaven and End Times

Lamb slain from the foundation of the world. ⁹ If any man have an ear, let him hear. ¹⁰ He that leadeth into captivity shall go into captivity: he that killeth with the sword must be killed with the sword. ***Here is the patience and the faith of the <u>saints</u>.***
Revelation 13:7-10

Another reason I believe there will be Christians on earth who will suffer the Tribulation is that incense (sweet-smelling smoke) often describes prayers going up. These prayers will be the prayers of saints present during the Tribulation. God also told the martyred to wait a little longer because not all their fellowservants and brethren had joined them in heaven.

And the smoke of the incense, which came with ***the prayers of the saints, ascended up*** before God out of the angel's hand.
Revelation 8:4

And they cried with a loud voice, saying, How long, O Lord, holy and true, dost thou not judge and avenge our blood on them that dwell on the earth? ¹¹ And white robes were given unto every one of them; and it was said unto them, that they should ***rest yet for a little season, until their fellowservants also and their brethren, that should be killed as they were, should be fulfilled.***
Revelation 6:10-11

Finally, we are also told that Satan will persecute Christians during the Tribulation. The woman below is symbolic for Christians.

Therefore rejoice, ye heavens, and ye that dwell in them. Woe to the inhabiters of the earth and of the sea! for the devil is come down unto you, having great wrath, because he knoweth that he hath but a short time. 13 And when the dragon saw that he was cast unto the earth, ***he persecuted the woman which brought forth the man child***
Revelation 12:12-13

1. Isaiah 13:9, God will lay the land desolate. What will God do to the sinners?

2. Mark 13:19, When will the Tribulation take place?

3. 2 Timothy 3:1-7, Name some of the clues regarding mankind that indicate that the End Times are close?

4. 2 Timothy 3:1-7, Do these verses describe mankind today?

5. Matthew 24:6, and Luke 21:11, What clues will we see in the world that the End Times are near?

Matthew 24:37-42

6. Verses 37-38, In the day of Noah did the people believe that the earth would be flooded?

7. Verses 24:39-42, Will they believe that Jesus is coming back?

8. Verses 40-41, What will happen when the rapture takes place?

9. Daniel 12:1, When the rapture takes place, what is the condition that one must meet to be raptured?

10. 1 Thessalonians 4:16-17, When the trump sounds, the dead in Christ and the remaining living in Christ will be caught up in the air. Who will we be with forever?

11. Revelation 13:7-10, The Antichrist is now on the scene. It is the beginning of the Tribulation period. Will these Christians go through the Tribulation?

12. Revelation 13:10, How do we know that these people are Christians? (Hint very last word).

Four Horses of Revelation and the Breaking of Seven Seals!

Is Jesus the rider on the white horse? Who breaks the seven seals? Who are the four beasts? What is the purpose of the four horses? What are the seven seals? Very fascinating questions.

Although Jesus will come later riding a white horse, he is not believed to be the rider of the first white horse. The Bible tells us that the Lamb (Jesus) opened the book of seals, but it does not mention him riding any of the four horses.

> And I saw when the Lamb opened one of the seals, and I heard, as it were the noise of thunder, one of the four beasts saying, Come and see.
>
> Revelation 6:1

The above four beasts are believed to be Seraphim Angels by their description given earlier in Revelation. They are "full of eyes in front and behind" and look to John like a lion, an ox, a man, and an eagle in flight. They also each have six wings full of eyes and their job is to worship God.

> And before the throne there was a sea of glass like unto crystal: and in the midst of the throne, and round about the throne, were four beasts full of eyes before and behind. [7] And the first beast was like a lion, and the second beast like a calf, and the third beast had a face as a man, and the fourth beast was like a flying eagle. [8] And the four beasts had each of them six wings about him; and they were full of eyes within: and they rest not day and night, saying, Holy, holy, holy, LORD God Almighty, which was, and is, and is to come.
>
> Revelation 4:6-8

It is believed that the four horses are symbolic of what will take place before the final judgement. They represent God's judgment of sin and rebellion and will take place in the first three and half years of the Tribulation. They will deliver the first four seals.

THE FOUR HORSES
- **White Horse** – The Antichrist (false messiah) will be ushered in
- **Red Horse** – The Antichrist will cause global warfare and bloodshed
- **Black Horse** – Global famine and death
- **Pale Horse** – Disease, animal attacks, and death of 1/4 of earth's population. This horseman is described as Death and Hell followed

him. No, there will not be two horsemen. The pale horseman is picking up the unsaved (dead in Christ) and sending them to Hades. Hades is the place where the unsaved wait to be judged.

> And I saw when the Lamb opened one of the seals, and I heard, as it were the noise of thunder, one of the four beasts saying, Come and see. ² And I saw, and behold *a white horse*: and he that sat on him had a bow; and a crown was given unto him: and he went forth *conquering, and to conquer*. ³ And when he had opened the second seal, I heard the second beast say, Come and see. ⁴ And there went out *another horse that was red*: and power was given to him that sat thereon to *take peace from the earth, and that they should kill one another:* and there was given unto him a great sword. ⁵ And when he had opened the third seal, I heard the third beast say, Come and see. And I beheld, and lo *a black horse*; and he that sat on him had a pair of balances in his hand. ⁶ And I heard a voice in the midst of the four beasts say, *A measure of wheat for a penny, and three measures of barley for a penny; and see thou hurt not the oil and the wine*. ⁷ And when he had opened the fourth seal, I heard the voice of the fourth beast say, Come and see. ⁸ And I looked, and behold *a pale horse*: and his name that sat on him was *Death, and Hell followed with him. And power was given unto them over the fourth part of the earth, to kill with sword, and with hunger, and with death, and with the beasts of the earth.*
>
> Revelation 6:1-8

Revelation is not the only book in the Bible to reference horses as judgment for man's sins. Zechariah 6:1-8 lists four chariots drawn by a red horse, black horse, white horse, and bay horse. They executed God's judgment and anger toward sin and the wicked.

The Four Horsemen events will take place at the beginning of the seven seals as you will see below.

THE SEVEN SEALS

1. **Antichrist** – the Antichrist will be ushered in by the breaking of this seal and delivered by the white horse. Some think this is Jesus, but many scholars believe each horse symbolizes judgement and a specific period of time. As you will see later the Antichrist will portray himself as God. He will be power-hungry and vain. He will seek power by getting rid of anyone who gets in his way.

> And I saw, and behold a *white horse*: and he that sat on him had a bow; and a crown was given unto him: and he went *forth conquering, and to conquer.*

Revelation 6:2

2. **<u>Warfare and Bloodshed</u>** – will be delivered by the Red Horse,

> And there went out another ***horse that was red***: and power was given to him that sat thereon to ***take peace from the earth***, and that ***they should kill one another***: and there was given unto him a great sword.
> Revelation 6:4

3. **<u>Famine and death</u>** – will be delivered by the black horse whose color represents death.

> And when he had opened the third seal, I heard the third beast say, Come and see. And I beheld, and lo ***a black horse***; and he that sat on him had a pair of balances in his hand. ⁶ And I heard a voice in the midst of the four beasts say, ***A measure of wheat for a penny, and three measures of barley for a penny***; and see thou hurt not the oil and the wine.
> Revelation 6:5-6

4. **<u>Disease, animal attacks, and death</u>** – will be delivered by the pale horse. This will be the death of one-fourth of the earth.

> And I looked, and behold ***a pale horse***: and his name that sat on him was ***Death, and Hell followed with him***. And power was given unto them over the fourth part of the earth, to ***kill with sword***, and ***with hunger***, and ***with death***, and ***with the beasts of the earth***.
> Revelation 6:8

5. **<u>The martyred in Heaven are given White Robes</u>** – the martyred are wanting to become part of the judgement but are encouraged by God to wait until those that are martyred during the Tribulation join them. They will later serve with Jesus in the Millennial.

> And when he had opened the fifth seal, I saw under the altar the souls of them that were slain for the word of God, and for the testimony which they held: ¹⁰ And they cried with a loud voice, saying, How long, O Lord, holy and true, dost thou not judge and avenge our blood on them that dwell on the earth? ¹¹ And white robes were given unto every one of them; and it was said unto them, that they should rest yet for a little season, until their fellowservants also and their brethren, that should be killed as they were, should be fulfilled.
> Revelation 6:9-11

6. **Catastrophic natural events** – worldwide earthquakes, the stars will fall from the sky, the sun will turn black, the moon blood-red, and the mountains and islands will disappear, and mighty winds will blow. Man will try to hide from God's wrath, but he will not succeed.

> And I beheld when he had opened the sixth seal, and, lo, there was a great earthquake; and the sun became black as sackcloth of hair, and the moon became as blood; [13] And the stars of heaven fell unto the earth, even as a fig tree casteth her untimely figs, when she is shaken of a mighty wind. [14] And the heaven departed as a scroll when it is rolled together; and every mountain and island were moved out of their places. [15] And the kings of the earth, and the great men, and the rich men, and the chief captains, and the mighty men, and every bondman, and every free man, hid themselves in the dens and in the rocks of the mountains; [16] And said to the mountains and rocks, Fall on us, and hide us from the face of him that sitteth on the throne, and from the wrath of the Lamb: [17] For the great day of his wrath is come; and who shall be able to stand?
> Revelation 6:12-17

7. **Silence in Heaven & censer of fire** – This symbolizes the sabbath day, a day of rest and worship of God. After the pause, the angel takes the container in which incense is burned to worship God, fills it with fire from the altar, and throws it to the earth. Following this, the seven trumpets will be revealed.

> And when he had opened the seventh seal, there was silence in heaven about the space of half an hour. 2 And I saw the seven angels which stood before God; and to them were given seven trumpets. 3 And another angel came and stood at the altar, having a golden censer; and there was given unto him much incense, that he should offer it with the prayers of all saints upon the golden altar which was before the throne. 4 And the smoke of the incense, which came with the prayers of the saints, ascended up before God out of the angel's hand. 5 And the angel took the censer, and filled it with fire of the altar, and cast it into the earth: and there were voices, and thunderings, and lightnings, and an earthquake.
> Revelation 8:1-5

I again encourage you if you are not saved or are not sure of your salvation, please seek help so you know for sure that you will not have to go through these terrible times.

Heaven and End Times

1. Revelation 6:1, Do you think it is Jesus who will open the seal? Explain your answer.

2. Revelation 6:1, Revelation 4:6-8, What do you believe the four beasts are?

3. Revelation 6:2, Why is this horseman thought to be the Antichrist?

4. Revelation 6:3-4, What is the job of the second horseman?

5. Revelation 6:5-6, What is the job of the third horseman?

6. Revelation 6:7-8, What is the job of the fourth horseman?

7. Revelation 6:2-17, and 8:5, Name the seven seals?

8. Revelation 8:1, Why do you think there was silence in Heaven on this seventh seal? Explain.

The Seven Trumpets You Do Not Want to Hear!

What is the purpose of the Seven Trumpets? Should people who hear the Trumpets be afraid? Who blows the trumpets? What are the Seven Trumpets?

The purpose of the Seven Trumpets is to warn that judgment is certain, so make yourself right with God. It will be a call for good and evil to battle (Armageddon). Most importantly they announce the return of Jesus. I am sure that you have seen depicted in movies where trumpets are blown to announce kings. Well, what king is as worthy as our King Jesus? None!

Should people who hear the Trumpets be afraid? Most definitely, especially those who still have not accepted Jesus as their Saviour. Their time to accept Jesus is about over. If they thought the seals were bad, they better be prepared for horrific times.

The seven Trumpets are ushered in after a period of rest, worship, and prayer at the end of the seventh seal. The martyrs in heaven are told to wait until their fellowservants (martyrs from the Tribulation) join them. When this happens God will avenge their pain.

> And they cried with a loud voice, saying, How long, O Lord, holy and true, dost thou not judge and avenge our blood on them that dwell on the earth? [11] And white robes were given unto every one of them; and it was said unto them, that they should *rest yet for a little season, until their fellowservants also and their brethren, that should be killed as they were, should be fulfilled.*
>
> Revelation 6:10-11

During the time of the seventh seal, we are told that prayers of saints came up to heaven as smoke. Just as our prayers are heard now, so will these saints (Christians), be heard. People can still turn their lives over to Jesus. However, as I stated earlier, they will go through terrible times, but they will have the peace of knowing they will be with Jesus in the end.

> And another angel came and stood at the altar, having a golden censer; and there was given unto him much incense, that *he should offer it with the prayers of all saints* upon the golden altar which was before the throne. 4 And the *smoke of the incense, which came with the prayers of the saints*, ascended up before God out of the angel's hand.
>
> Revelation 8:3-4

So, who will sound the trumpets? The answer is seven of God's angels,

> And I saw *the seven angels which stood before God; and to them were given seven trumpets*…⁵And the angel took the censer, and filled it with fire of the altar, and cast it into the earth: and there were voices, and thunderings, and lightnings, and an earthquake. ⁶And the seven angels which had the seven trumpets prepared themselves to sound.
> Revelation 8:2,5-6

THE SEVEN TRUMPETS

1. Devastation of 1/3 part of the land –
> The first angel sounded, and there followed hail and fire mingled with blood, and they were cast upon the earth: and the third part of trees was burnt up, and all green grass was burnt up.
> Revelation 8:7

2. Devastation of 1/3 of the sea –
> And the second angel sounded, and as it were a great mountain burning with fire was cast into the sea: and the third part of the sea became blood; 9 And the third part of the creatures which were in the sea, and had life, died; and the third part of the ships were destroyed.
> Revelation 8:8-9

3. Devastation of 1/3 of freshwater –
> And the third angel sounded, and there fell a great star from heaven, burning as it were a lamp, and it fell upon the third part of the rivers, and upon the fountains of waters; 11 And the name of the star is called **Wormwood**: and the third part of the waters became wormwood; and many men died of the waters, because they were **made bitter**.
> Revelation 8:10-11

4. Devastation of 1/3 of the sky –
> And the fourth angel sounded, and the third part of the sun was smitten, and the third part of the moon, and the third part of the stars; so as the third part of them was darkened, and the day shone not for a third part of it, and the night likewise.
> Revelation 8:12

5. Monster locusts inflict suffering on the unsaved – (*Note the description of the locust starting in verse 7. I find them extremely scary.*)

And the fifth angel sounded, and I saw a star fall from heaven unto the earth: and to him was given the key of the bottomless pit. 2 And he opened the bottomless pit; and there arose a smoke out of the pit, as the smoke of a great furnace; and the sun and the air were darkened by reason of the smoke of the pit. 3 And there came out of the smoke *locusts* upon the earth: and unto them was given *power, as the scorpions* of the earth have power. And it was commanded them that ***they should not hurt the grass of the earth, neither any green thing, neither any tree; but only those men which have not the seal of God in their foreheads.*** 5 And to them it was given that they should not kill them, but that ***they should be tormented five months***: and their torment was as the torment of a scorpion, when he striketh a man. ***6 And in those days shall men seek death, and shall not find it; and shall desire to die, and death shall flee from them.*** 7 And the shapes of the locusts were like unto horses prepared unto battle; and on their heads were as it were crowns like gold, and their faces were as the faces of men. 8 And they had hair as the hair of women, and their teeth were as the teeth of lions. 9 And they had breastplates, as it were breastplates of iron; and the sound of their wings was as the sound of chariots of many horses running to battle. 10 And they had tails like unto scorpions, and there were stings in their tails: and their power was to hurt men five months. 11 And they had a king over them, which is the angel of the bottomless pit, whose name in the Hebrew tongue is Abaddon, but in the Greek tongue hath his name Apollyon.

Revelation 9:1-11

6. Devastation of 1/3 of the human population (Yet the survivors will not repent) –

And the sixth angel sounded, and I heard a voice from the four horns of the golden altar which is before God, 14 Saying to the sixth angel which had the trumpet, Loose the four angels which are bound in the great river Euphrates. 15 And the four angels were loosed, which were prepared for an hour, and a day, and a month, and a year, for to slay the third part of men. 16 And the number of the army of the horsemen were two hundred thousand: and I heard the number of them. 17 And thus I saw the horses in the vision, and them that sat on them, having breastplates of fire, and of jacinth, and brimstone: and the heads of the horses were as the heads of lions; and out of their mouths issued fire and smoke and brimstone. 18 By these three was the third part of men killed, by the fire, and by the smoke, and by the brimstone, which issued out of their mouths. 19 For their power is in their mouth, and in their tails: for their tails were like unto serpents, and had heads, and with them they do hurt.

Revelation 9:13-19

7. Jesus reclaims his place as King (lightnings, voices, thunderings, earthquake, and hail) –

And the seventh angel sounded; and there were great voices in heaven, saying, ***The kingdoms of this world are become the kingdoms of our Lord, and of his Christ; and he shall reign for ever and ever.*** 16 And the four and twenty elders, which sat before God on their seats, fell upon their faces, and worshipped God, 17 Saying, We give thee thanks, O Lord God Almighty, which art, and wast, and art to come; because thou hast taken to thee thy great power, and hast reigned. 18 And the nations were angry, and thy wrath is come, and the time of the dead, that they should be judged, and that thou shouldest give reward unto thy servants the prophets, and to the saints, and them that fear thy name, small and great; and shouldest destroy them which destroy the earth. 19 And the temple of God was opened in heaven, and there was seen in his temple the ark of his testament: and there were lightnings, and voices, and thunderings, and an earthquake, and great hail.

Revelation 11:15-19

Many are fooled by the philosophy that God is a loving God and will let everyone into heaven. He is indeed a loving God and gives each person, right up to the last moment, a chance to repent and accept Jesus as their Saviour. It is not God that brings these things upon us, it is man who thinks he can eat his cake and have it too. We must decide who we are going to serve and honor. Choices come with consequences.

1. Revelation 6:10-11, Why was the martyred in Christ told to wait?

2. Revelation 8:7, What does this trumpet usher in?

3. Revelation 8:8-9, What does this trumpet usher in?

4. Revelation 8:10-11, What does this trumpet usher in?

5. Revelation 8:12, What does this trumpet usher in?

6. Revelation 9:1-11, What does this trumpet usher in?

7. Revelation 9:5, How long will the locust inflict pain?

8. Revelation 9:6, What will the tortured people wish?

9. Revelation 9:13-19, What does this trumpet usher in?

10. Revelation 11:15-19, What does this trumpet usher in?

Antichrists!

When we think of the word Antichrist, we automatically think of End Times but, there are many Antichrists. An Antichrist can be singular or plural. *Oxford Dictionaries-Bing Translator* defines Antichrist as, [1]"a personal opponent of Christ expected to appear before the end of the world. A person or force seen as opposing Christ or the Christian Church. A person or thing regarded as supremely evil or as a fundamental enemy or opponent."

I would like to point out one important fact; if there is not a Christ then why would there be a need for an Antichrist? Think about it, have you ever posted a Christian post and received backlash from family or friends? Have you ever read some of the comments left on famous Christian leaders' posts, such as Franklin Graham? If there is no Christ, then exactly what makes these people see red?

The reason I believe many get upset at the mere mention of Christ is because they know in their hearts there is a Christ but do not want to let go of their sins. They are under the misconception that life is over if they accept Jesus as their savior; but really life has just begun. We love deeper, laugh, joke, work, play, and enjoy life with the knowledge and peace of mind that someday we will be with Jesus.

There are many Antichrists already in our world,

> And every spirit that confesseth not that Jesus Christ is come in the flesh is not of God: and this is that spirit of antichrist, whereof ye have heard that it should come; and ***even now already is it in the world.***
>
> 1 John 4:3

One important characteristic is always prominent in an Antichrist. They deny that Jesus is Christ (God's Son)

> Who is a liar but he that denieth that Jesus is the Christ? ***He is antichrist, that denieth the Father and the Son.***
>
> 1 John 2:22

> For many deceivers are entered into the world, ***who confess not that Jesus Christ is come in the flesh.*** This is a deceiver and an antichrist.
>
> 2 John 1:7

What is the purpose of Antichrist(s)? Mainly to keep people from accepting Jesus as their savior but also to confuse those who are saved (but not strong in God's word). The Antichrist will use these people's influence to manipulate the unsaved into believing they need to follow the Antichrist. The Bible confirms that many will be led astray even Christians (elect).

> For false Christs and false prophets shall rise, and shall shew signs and wonders, to seduce, if it were possible, ***even the elect***.
> Mark 13:22

How in the world could a Christian be fooled? The answer is quite simple, failure to study God's word continuously.

> But strong meat belongeth to them that are of full age, even those ***who by reason of use have their senses exercised to discern both good and evil.***
> Hebrews 5:14

As Christians, we should always check out our Pastor's messages. It is our job to make sure the truth is taught from the pulpit and that a true man of God is filling our pulpits. Many Churches look at promising resumes, but promising resumes do not always reflect the true person.

> ***Study to shew thyself approved unto God***, a workman that needeth not to be ashamed, ***rightly dividing the word of truth.***
> 2 Timothy 2:15

> ***Beware of false prophets***, which come to you in sheep's clothing, but inwardly they are ravening wolves.
> Matthew 7:15

In conclusion, there are false prophets and Antichrists in the world today. We have been warned and it is our duty to detect them and weed them from prominent positions.

---

[1]Oxford Languages · Bing Translator, Antichrist, as of December 22, 2022

Heaven and End Times

1. What does the word Antichrist mean?

2. 1 John 4:3, Are there Antichrist in the world today?

3. 1 John 2:22, and 2 John 1:7 What is a characteristic that is always found in an Antichrist?

4. What is the purpose of Antichrists?

5. Mark 13:22, Who does the Antichrist lead astray?

6. Mark 13:22, How does the Antichrist lead these people astray?

7. Hebrews 5:14, How is it possible to lead a Christian astray?

8. 2 Timothy 2:15, Tells us we should study God's word. What do you think, "rightly dividing the word of truth", means?

9. Matthew 7:15, Is every man behind the pulpit a true man of God? Explain.

10. Is it the congregation's job to make sure their pastor, minister, etc. are true men of God? Explain why it is important to make sure the truth is preached?

The Antichrist!

In the previous chapter, we talked about Antichrists that will be present from the time of Jesus' death until his return (End Times). But the Antichrist that ushers in the Tribulation will be so much more deceitful, and powerful than any of the other Antichrists.

When will this all-powerful Antichrist come? Paul says there must be a falling away (rebellion) first,

> Let no man deceive you by any means: for that day shall not come, ***except there come a falling away first, and that man of sin be revealed, the son of perdition;***
>
> 2 Thessalonians 2:3

The Bible tells us what we will see during this time of rebellion,

> This know also, that in the last days perilous times shall come. 2 For men shall be lovers of their own selves, covetous, boasters, proud, blasphemers, disobedient to parents, unthankful, unholy, 3 Without natural affection, trucebreakers, false accusers, incontinent, fierce, despisers of those that are good, 4 Traitors, heady, highminded, lovers of pleasures more than lovers of God; 5 Having a form of godliness, but denying the power thereof: from such turn away.
>
> 2 Timothy 3:1-5

The earth and sky will also show us signs,

> But when ye shall hear of wars and commotions, be not terrified: for these things must first come to pass; but the end is not by and by. 10 Then said he unto them, Nation shall rise against nation, and kingdom against kingdom: 11 And great earthquakes shall be in divers places, and famines, and pestilences; and fearful sights and great signs shall there be from heaven.
>
> Luke 21:9-11

2 Thessalonians informs us that the name of the man of sin (the son of perdition) would be revealed at the End Times. This son of perdition will be

the Antichrist. He and Judas are the only men in the Bible called sons of perdition. Judas served his purpose as will the Antichrist.

> Let no man deceive you by any means: for that day shall not come, except there come a falling away first, ***and that man of sin be revealed, the son of perdition;***
> 2 Thessalonians 2:3

BibleVerseStudy.com defines son of Perdition as follows: [1]"απωλειας *(apoleias)*, the original Greek word translated **"of perdition,"** means "of destruction" or "of ruin," so **"the son of perdition"** means the son of destruction or ruin."

The Antichrist will set himself up as being God and will expect people to worship him as God.

> Who opposeth and exalteth himself above all that is called God, or that is worshipped; so that he as God sitteth in the temple of God, ***shewing himself that he is God.***
> 2 Thessalonians 2:4

Jesus warned us of the above before he left:

> Then if any man shall say unto you, Lo, here is Christ, or there; believe it not.
> Matthew 24:23

So, why will the people follow the Antichrist? They will follow him because he will have powers never seen before.

> Even him, whose coming is after the working of Satan ***with all power and signs and lying wonders,*** 10 And with all deceivableness of unrighteousness in them that perish; because they received not the love of the truth, that they might be saved.
> 2 Thessalonians 2:9-10

---

[1]"SON OF PERDITION" - Who Is He And Why Is He Called That? (bibleversestudy.com), John 17:12-13 Son of Perdition, As of December 22, 2021.

1. 2 Thessalonians 2:3, What must happen before the last Antichrist comes?

2. 2 Thessalonians 2:3, Who will be revealed?

3. What does the son of perdition mean?

4. John 17:12, What does Jesus call Judas in this verse?

5. 2 Timothy 3:1-5, List the people's behaviors during this time of rebellion?

6. Luke 21:10-11, What will happen before End Times?

7. 2 Thessalonians 2:4, Who will the Antichrist project himself as being?

8. Matthew 24:23, Did Jesus warn us that someone would falsely say they were him?

9. 2 Thessalonians 2:9-10, How will this Antichrist mislead people?

10. 2 Thessalonians 2:10, What will happen to the people who believe and worship him?

The Entrance of the Antichrist!

We know that the Antichrist will declare himself mightier than God. He will set himself up to be worshiped in God's temple. Many Christians take this literally as do I. I believe that God's Temple will be rebuilt a third time.

> Who opposeth and exalteth himself above all that is called God, or that is worshipped; so that he as God sitteth in the temple of God, ***shewing himself that he is God***.
>
> 2 Thessalonians 2:4

It is said that preparations for the third temple have already started. In fact, according to an article in Messianic Prophecy Bible Project, [1]"the furnishings, musical instruments, and vessels for Temple worship have already been created and are on display at the Treasures of the Temple exhibition in Jerusalem."

The wording in the UAE-Israel accord states, [2]"As set forth in the Vision for Peace, all Muslims who come in peace may visit and pray at Al Aqsa Mosque, and Jerusalem's other holy sites should remain open for peaceful worshippers of all faiths." Before this Jews were not allowed to worship there.

Satan will mimic the Holy Trinity (God, Jesus, and Holy Spirit). His trinity will consist of (Satan, the Antichrist, and the False Prophet). The Antichrist will be a political leader more than likely coming out of the old Roman Empire. It is said he will be a Gentile because of the reference of the beast coming out of the Sea.

> And I stood upon the sand of the sea, and ***saw a beast rise up out of the sea,*** having seven heads and ten horns, and upon his horns ten crowns, and upon his heads the name of blasphemy.
>
> Revelation 13:1

The name of blasphemy will be the act of calling himself God and expecting people to worship him. The description of the beast represents the magnitude of the authority of weapons, power, and dominion he has over kings and nations. After the introduction of a mystery woman, we will see how we arrive at this statement.

> [3] So he carried me away in the spirit into the wilderness: and I saw a woman sit upon a ***scarlet coloured beast***, full of names of blasphemy, having seven heads and ten horns. [4] And the woman

was arrayed in purple and scarlet colour, and decked with gold and precious stones and pearls, having a golden cup in her hand full of abominations and filthiness of her fornication: ⁵ And upon her forehead was a name written, MYSTERY, BABYLON THE GREAT, THE MOTHER OF HARLOTS AND ABOMINATIONS OF THE EARTH. ⁶ And I saw the woman drunken with the blood of the saints, and with the blood of the martyrs of Jesus: and when I saw her, I wondered with great admiration.

Revelation 17:3-6

The beast in Revelation 17:3 is the Antichrist. But who is this woman mentioned in the above verses? Back in Biblical days women often advertised that they were harlots by writing across their foreheads. They would adorn themselves with jewelry and fine clothing. This harlot will appear to be beautiful but inside she is rotten to her core. She has prostituted herself to Satan. She will entice people to worship the Antichrist. She will be every sin that God hates (Abominations of the earth).

The Bible tells us not to marvel at this woman:

⁷ And the angel said unto me, **_Wherefore didst thou marvel?_** I will tell thee the mystery of the woman, and of the beast that carrieth her, which hath the seven heads and ten horns. ⁸ The beast that thou sawest was, and is not; and shall ascend out of the bottomless pit, and go into perdition: and they that dwell on the earth shall wonder, whose names were not written in the book of life from the foundation of the world, when they behold the beast that was, and is not, and yet is.

Revelation 17:7-8

The seven heads are described as seven mountains that the harlot sits on. It is thought that this symbolizes a huge city that sits on top of seven mountains. The ten horns are kings.

⁹ And here is the mind which hath wisdom. **_The seven heads are seven mountains, on which the woman sitteth_**.

Revelation 17:9

¹² And **_the ten horns which thou sawest are ten kings_**, which have received no kingdom as yet; but receive power as kings one hour with the beast.

Revelation 17:12

When the beast first appears on the scene notice how he is described:

> And the beast which I saw was like unto a ***leopard***, and his feet were as the ***feet of a bear***, and his mouth as the ***mouth of a lion***:
>
> Revelation 13:2a

A leopard omits a sweet popcorn scent that attracts prey. The Antichrist will also lure the world to himself, and many will become his prey. A leopard is extremely swift and like the swiftness of the leopard, the Antichrist will swiftly come to power. Also, leopards have spots that represent sin.

The feet of a bear implies strength and the ability to destroy, tear, and shred all that gets in his way.

The mouth of a lion instills a picture of a roaring lion. It causes fear to all who hear it. It also symbolizes a mouth full of sharp teeth devouring its prey. The Antichrist will take your property, possessions and kill anyone who gets in his way.

But who gives him this power? The dragon in the following verse refers to Satan himself.

> and the ***dragon*** gave him his power, and his seat, and great authority.
>
> Revelation 13:2b

The Antichrist will fake a resurrection to declare himself as being the Messiah.

> ***And I saw one of his heads as it were wounded to death; and his deadly wound was healed: and all the world wondered after the beast.*** 4 And they worshipped the dragon which gave power unto the beast: and they worshipped the beast, saying, Who is like unto the beast? who is able to make war with him?
>
> Revelation 13:3-4

Following this fake resurrection, there will be a 3 1/2 year war on Christians.

> [5]And there was given unto him a mouth speaking great things and blasphemies; ***and power was given unto him to continue forty and two months***...[7]And it was given unto ***him to make war with the saints, and to overcome them:*** and power was given him over all kindreds, and tongues, and nations. [8] And all that dwell upon the earth shall worship him, whose names are not written in the book of life of the Lamb slain from the foundation of the world.
>
> Revelation 13:5,7-8

During the time of the Antichrist, people will feel the full wrath of Satan. The woman in the following verses symbolizes Christians. Pay special attention to verse 13,

> Therefore rejoice, ye heavens, and ye that dwell in them. Woe to the inhabiters of the earth and of the sea! for the devil is come down unto you, having great wrath, because he knoweth that he hath but a short time. 13 And when the dragon saw that he was cast unto the earth, ***he persecuted the woman which brought forth the man child***
>
> Revelation 12:12-13

At this point, the rapture has already taken place. The Antichrist will be powered by Satan. Christians (people saved after the rapture) will be persecuted.

References

[1] The Temple Vessels Are Ready for the Rebuilding of Jerusalem's Third Temple | Messianic Bible, The Messianic Prophecy Bible Project, The Temple Vessels Are Ready for the Rebuilding of Jerusalem's Third Temple, As of December 22, 2021

[2] https://www.israel365news.com/157777/how-uae-peace-deal-brings-temple-mount-prophecy-life/#:~:text="As%20set%20forth%20in%20the%20Vision%20for%20Peace%2C,plan%20concerning%20relations%20between%20the%20Palestinians%20and%20Israel.
TRUMP'S ABRAHAM ACCORDS BRINGS TRUE SONS OF ISHMAEL TO TEMPLE MT AS PROPHESIED IN ZOHAR, BY ADAM ELIYAHU BERKOWITZ | SEP 2, 2020 | BIBLICAL NEWS

Heaven and End Times

1. 2 Thessalonians 2:4, Who does the Antichrist think he is above?

2. Isaiah 14:12-15, Who was thrown out of Heaven and why?

3. Revelation 13:1, What do seven heads, ten horns, and ten crowns represent?

4. Revelation 13:1, What does, "upon his heads the name of blasphemy", mean?

5. Revelation 13:2a, What are the three characteristics of the Antichrist and their meanings?

6. Revelation 13:2b, Who gives the Antichrist his power and authority?

7. Revelation 13:8, What is the spiritual condition of the people who worship the Antichrist?

8. Revelation 12:12, What is the woe warning, and who does it pertain to?

9. Revelation 12:13, Who was the woman that brought forth the man child?

10. Revelation 17:3, Who is the beast in this verse?

11. Revelation 17:5, What is written on this woman's head?

12. Revelation 17:5, What does Abominations of the Earth mean?

13. Revelation 17:7, Should we marvel at this woman?

14. Revelation 17:9, What do the seven heads represent?

15. Revelation 17:12, What do the ten horns represent?

The Seven Years of the Antichrist and the Seven Vials of God's Wrath!

We often hear of the seven years of the Antichrist (Tribulation), but the Bible does not provide this information for us all in one place. This makes it very difficult to understand. The books of Daniel and Revelation contain a lot of information regarding these subjects. These books describe them as things to come. Things to come are considered Bible Prophecy. Often the Bible uses symbols when speaking of prophecy.

Daniel tells us that during the ushering in of the Tribulation period, there will be a 7-year covenant (peace treaty) for Israel, but it will be broken by the Antichrist halfway through (3 ½ years). Please note that the one week talked about in Daniel is seven years (each day is a year).

> And he shall confirm the ***covenant with many for one week: and in the midst of the week*** he shall cause the sacrifice and the oblation to cease, and for the overspreading of abominations he shall make it desolate, even until the consummation, and that determined shall be poured upon the desolate.
>
> Daniel 9:27

During the first 3 ½ years the Antichrist will exalt himself as a peacemaker while seating himself up to rule the world. He will woo the ten kings (horns) to serve him and his cause. Later these kings will turn their kingdoms and power over to the Antichrist in a ridiculously short amount of time.

> And the ten horns which thou sawest are ***ten kings***, which have received no kingdom as yet; but receive power as kings ***one hour*** with the beast. 13 These have one mind, and ***shall give their power and strength unto the beast.***
>
> Revelation 17:12-13

The Antichrist will set himself up as God.

> And there was given unto him a mouth speaking great things and blasphemies; and power was given unto him to continue ***forty and two month***...[8]And all that dwell upon the earth ***shall worship him***, whose names are not written in the book of life of the Lamb slain from the foundation of the world.
>
> Revelation 13:5,8

The Antichrist will claim God's Temple as his own.

> And he shall speak great words against the most High, and shall wear out the saints of the most High, and think to change times and laws: and they shall be given into his hand until a time and times and the dividing of time.
>
> Daniel 7:25

The Antichrist will make war against Christians,

> And it was given unto him to make war with the saints, and to overcome them: and power was given him over all kindreds, and tongues, and nations.
>
> Revelation 13:7

People will be forced to take on the mark of the beast. If they do not, they will be persecuted.

> And he causeth all, both small and great, rich and poor, free and bond, to receive a mark in their right hand, or in their foreheads: 17 And that no man might buy or sell, save he that had the mark, or the name of the beast, or the number of his name.
>
> Revelation 13:16-17

When Jesus talked about End Times he said there never was or will be a time as bad as the rule under the Antichrist. No one will escape the tribulation unless they are saved (elect).

> For then shall be great ***Tribulation, such as was not since the beginning of the world to this time, no, nor ever shall be***. 22 And except those days should be shortened, there should no flesh be saved: but for the elect's sake those days shall be shortened. 23 Then if any man shall say unto you, Lo, here is Christ, or there; believe it not. 24 For there shall arise false Christs, and false prophets, and shall shew great signs and wonders; insomuch that, if it were possible, they shall deceive the very elect.
>
> Matthew 24:21-24

The earth's population will undergo seven (plagues)/vial judgements. These judgements are what Jesus meant when he said things would be worse than anything man has ever known or will know afterward.

The Vials of God's wrath

1. Troublesome and evil sores:

> And the first went, and poured out his vial upon the earth; and there fell a noisome and grievous sore upon the men which had the mark of the beast, and upon them which worshipped his image.
>
> Revelation 16:2

2. The Sea becomes blood:

   And the second angel poured out his vial upon the sea; and it became as the blood of a dead man: and every living soul died in the sea.

   Revelation 16:3

3. Rivers and springs become as blood:

   And the third angel poured out his vial upon the rivers and fountains of waters; and they became blood.

   Revelation 16:4

4. Power is given to the sun to scorch men:

   And the fourth angel poured out his vial upon the sun; and power was given unto him to scorch men with fire.

   Revelation 16:8

5. On the throne of the Antichrist was darkness and pain:

   And the fifth angel poured out his vial upon the seat of the beast; and his kingdom was full of darkness; and they gnawed their tongues for pain, 11 And blasphemed the God of heaven because of their pains and their sores, and repented not of their deeds.

   Revelation 16:10-11

6. The Euphrates River will dry up. With this river dry, invading armies will be able to cross over to battle.

   And the sixth angel poured out his vial upon the great river Euphrates; and the water thereof was dried up, that the way of the kings of the east might be prepared.

   Revelation 16:12

7. Plague of hail:

   [17]And the seventh angel poured out his vial into the air; and there came a great voice out of the temple of heaven, from the throne, saying, It is done... [21] And there fell upon men a great hail out of heaven, every stone about the weight of a talent: and men blasphemed God because of the plague of the hail; for the plague thereof was exceeding great.

   Revelation 16:17, 21

I do not know about you, but I am glad I am a child of God and will be raptured out before this misery takes place.

Daniel 9:27

1. What was made for one week?

2. Scholars say that one week is how long of time?

3. What ceases halfway through this agreement?

4. Revelation 17:12-13, How long do the ten kings keep their power and who do they give their power to?

5. Revelation 13:5 and 8, How long will the Antichrist continue to be in power and what will the people do?

6. Daniel 7:25, The Antichrist will speak against God. He will try to change what?

7. Matthew 24-21, What will happen and how bad will it be?

8. Matthew 24:22, What does "for the elect's sake those days shall be shortened" mean?

9. Revelation 13:7, What will the Antichrist do?

10. Revelation 16:2-21, What are the seven Vials of God's wrath?

The Antichrist and the False Prophet join forces!

The Antichrist has broken the 7-year covenant. He has committed war on those who have chosen Christ since the rapture. The living conditions are very bleak and dismal. Knowing this apostle John gives words of encouragement to help those Christians that were saved after the Rapture to hold onto their faith.

> If any man have an ear, let him hear. 10 He that leadeth into captivity shall go into captivity: he that killeth with the sword must be killed with the sword. *Here is the patience and the faith of the saints*.
>
> Revelation 13:9-10

We saw in one of the previous chapters that the Antichrist fakes his resurrection. He knew when Jesus died on the cross, was buried, and rose again, that he defeated his master (Satan), however; now the Antichrist seeks to deceive the world. He still thinks he can win against God. He will now be accompanied by the False Prophet whose mission is to destroy any trace of God.

The Antichrist will be a political power, but the False Prophet will be a man that mimics Christ's powers. He will perform miracles, but he will speak harshly like Satan.

> And I beheld *another beast* coming up out of the earth; and he had two horns like a lamb, and he spake as a dragon. 12 And he exerciseth all the power of the first beast before him, and c*auseth the earth and them which dwell therein to worship the first beast*, whose deadly wound was healed. 13 And *he doeth great wonders, so that he maketh fire come down from heaven on the earth in the sight of men,*
>
> Revelation 13:11-13

The False Prophet's main job will be to cause people to worship the Antichrist as stated above in verse 12. He will force upon the people a one-world religion that denies Christ.

> And deceiveth them that dwell on the earth by the means of those miracles which he had power to do in the sight of the beast; saying

to them that dwell on the earth, that they should make an image to
the beast, which had the wound by a sword, and did live.
Revelation 13:14

One of the False Prophets' powers will be that he can make an idol not only talk but also dish out punishment (murder) to any that will not worship the idol of the Antichrist.

And he had power to give life unto the image of the beast, that the image of the beast should both speak, and cause that as many as would not worship the image of the beast should be killed.
Revelation 13:15

The False Prophet will also require everyone to receive the mark of the beast on their right hand or forehead. Some will not and will be beheaded. Apostle John later sees these martyrs in his vision,

And I saw thrones, and they sat upon them, and judgment was given unto them: and I saw the souls of them that were beheaded for the witness of Jesus, and for the word of God, and which had not worshipped the beast, neither his image, neither had received his mark upon their foreheads, or in their hands; and they lived and reigned with Christ a thousand years.
Revelation 20:4

The good news is, the Antichrist and False Prophet are Satan's instruments of destruction, they are but men and will be thrown into the Lake of Fire at the Battle of Armageddon.

And I saw the beast, and the kings of the earth, and their armies, gathered together to make war against him that sat on the horse, and against his army.20 And the beast was taken, and with him the false prophet that wrought miracles before him, with which he deceived them that had received the mark of the beast, and them that worshipped his image. These both were cast alive into a lake of fire burning with brimstone.
Revelation 19:19-20

1. Revelation 13:9, When God says, "If any man have an ear, let him hear." Do you think it is something very important that he wants them to hear?

2. Revelation 13:10, These are words of _____ for the saints?

Revelation 13:11-14

3. Whose powers does the False Prophet try to mimic?

4. In verse 12, What does this False Prophet try to do?

5. In verse 13, What does the False Prophet make happen?

6. In verse 14, What must the people make?

7. Leviticus 26:1, What does God say about idols?

8. Revelation 13:15, What power did the False Prophet give to the image of the beast?

9. Revelation 20:4, What will happen to those who do not take the mark of the beast?

10. Revelation 19:20, What happens to the beast and the false prophet?

Mark of the Beast 666

Have you ever been someplace, and a person is given a bill for $6.66 and they say, "make it $6.67, 666 is bad, it is the mark of the beast"? No, it is not, the Bible clearly says that the mark of the beast will be "***IN***" the right hand or "***IN***" a person's forehead. It does not say it will be in a plate number, or a bill amount, or even a room number, etc.

> And he causeth all, both small and great, rich and poor, free and bond, to *receive a mark in their right hand, or in their foreheads:*
> Revelation 13:16

Revelation also tells us that without the mark of the beast you will not be able to buy or sell merchandise. In other words, if the beast does not kill you, your life will very rough. There will only be *3 ways* you can buy or sell. Please note that the mark is not just a number as many people will have you believe but can be (three) different kinds of marks (with the same meaning):

> And that no man might buy or sell, save he that had the *MARK*, or the *NAME* of the beast, or the *NUMBER* of his name.
> Revelation 13:17

- ACTUAL MARK OF SOME KIND
- NAME OF THE BEAST
- NUMBER OF HIS NAME:
  Here is wisdom. Let him that hath understanding count the number of the beast: for it is the number of a man; and his number is Six hundred threescore and six.
  Revelation 13:18

WHAT HAPPENS IF YOU ACCEPT THE MARK OF THE BEAST?

Be advised, the little bit of profit/comfort you get on earth by giving into the Antichrist (Beast) is not worth what God will do to you. Read these verses very carefully:

> And the third angel followed them, saying with a loud voice, ***If any man worship the beast and his image, and receive his mark in his forehead, or in his hand***, [10] The same shall drink of the wine of the wrath of God, which is poured out without mixture into the cup of his indignation; and he shall be tormented with fire and brimstone in the presence of the holy angels, and in the presence of the Lamb: [11] And the smoke of their torment ascendeth up for ever and

ever: and they have no rest day nor night, who worship the beast and his image, and whosoever receiveth the mark of his name.

Revelation 14:9-11

And I heard a great voice out of the temple saying to the seven angels, Go your ways, and pour out the vials of the wrath of God upon the earth. ² And the first went, and poured out his vial upon the earth; *and there fell a noisome and grievous sore upon the men which had the mark of the beast, and upon them which worshipped his image*.

Revelation 16:1-2

And the beast was taken, and with him the false prophet that wrought miracles before him, with which he deceived them that had received the mark of the beast, *and them that worshipped his image*. These both were cast alive into a lake of fire burning with brimstone.

Revelation 19:20

WHAT HAPPENS TO THOSE WHO *DO NOT* ACCEPT THE MARK?

They will live a very tough life on earth, some will be murdered, some will starve, some will be beaten half to death...but what God does for them after the great testing is marvelous! Notice below they will stand on the sea of glass. What does God's throne sit on? Yup, a sea of glass!

And I saw another sign in heaven, great and marvellous, seven angels having the seven last plagues; for in them is filled up the wrath of God. ²*And I saw as it were a sea of glass mingled with fire: and them that had gotten the victory over the beast, and over his image, and over his mark, and over the number of his name, <u>stand on the sea of glass, having the harps of God.</u>³ And they sing the song of Moses the servant of God, and the song of the Lamb, saying, Great and marvellous are thy works, Lord God Almighty; just and true are thy ways, thou King of saints.*

Revelation 15:1-3

And I saw thrones, and they sat upon them, and judgment was given unto them: and I saw the souls of them that were beheaded for the witness of Jesus, and for the word of God, and which had not worshipped the beast, neither his image, neither had received his mark upon their foreheads, or in their hands; and *they lived and reigned with Christ a thousand years*.

Revelation 20:4

Even the hardships one would suffer, they would be better off NOT TO ACCEPT THE MARK, because their eternal lives sound a whole lot nicer than the ones that, DO ACCEPT THE MARK. I would rather sing praises to God and reign with Jesus than eternity in the Lake of Fire.

1. Revelation 13:16, Where will the mark of the beast be on a person's body?

2. Revelation 13:17, To buy and sell anything what must you have?

3. Revelation 13:17, What are the three ways a person can receive the mark?

4. 2 Thessalonians 2:3, Revelation 13:18, We will find out the Antichrist's name during the Tribulation. What will the number of his name add up to?

5. Isaiah 14:13-14, 2 Thessalonians 2:3-4, Why do you think the Antichrist wants people to mark themselves?

6. Revelation 14:9-11, Revelation 16:1-2, and Revelation 19:20, What will happen to those who take the mark of the beast?

7. Revelation 15:1-3, 20:4, What will happen to those who do not take the mark of the beast?

8. Do you believe the mark of the Beast can be a room number, plate number, or bill amount? Explain.

Is The Second Coming and the Rapture the Same Thing!

We are taught of the second coming of Christ. But many use verses that depict the rapture of the church, not his return with the church. Think about it, how can Jesus come back both before and during the Tribulation? Nothing is mentioned about a third coming. What is the difference between the rapture and Jesus' second coming? Why is he going to come back? What will happen when he returns? Should we look forward to this time? A good Christian should seek the answers to these questions.

People often confuse the rapture of the church with Jesus returning with his church. The rapture makes no mention of Jesus touching his feet on the ground. We are told we will meet him in the air. In his second coming, he will battle on the earth in person, not in the air.

> But I would not have you to be ignorant, brethren, concerning them which are asleep, that ye sorrow not, even as others which have no hope. 14 For if we believe that Jesus died and rose again, even so them also which sleep in Jesus will God bring with him. 15 For this we say unto you by the word of the Lord, that we which are alive and remain unto the coming of the Lord shall not prevent them which are asleep. *16 For the Lord himself shall descend from heaven with a shout, with the voice of the archangel, and with the trump of God: and the dead in Christ shall rise first: 17 Then we which are alive and remain shall be caught up together with them in the clouds, to meet the Lord in the air: and so shall we ever be with the Lord.* 18 Wherefore comfort one another with these word.
>
> 1 Thessalonians 4:13-18

The above verse simply tells us not to mourn long for the dead because they shall rise, along with those alive in Christ, and will meet together with Jesus in the sky. This is called by Christians, "The Rapture!". The unsaved will be left behind to go through the Tribulation. The Antichrist will have to tell a great lie to cover this up.

Jesus promised to receive (rapture) us. At this time, he will be taking us to our mansion not to battle on the earth.

> Let not your heart be troubled: ye believe in God, believe also in me. 2 In my Father's house are many mansions: if it were not so, I would have told you. I go to prepare a place for you. 3 And if I go and prepare a place for you, *I will come again, and receive you unto myself; that where I am, there ye may be also.*
>
> John 14:1-3

We are told by God's word to look for the coming (rapture) of Jesus. We are also told to get our house in order which simply means make sure our family knows Jesus so they will not experience the Tribulation.

> Watch therefore: for ye know not what hour your Lord doth come. 43 But know this, that if the goodman of the house had known in what watch the thief would come, he would have watched, and would not have suffered his house to be broken up. 44 Therefore be ye also ready: for in such an hour as ye think not the Son of man cometh.
> Matthew 24:42-44

Jesus will come on a white horse for his second coming. When we are raptured there is no white horse.

> And I saw heaven opened, and behold a white horse; and he that sat upon him was called Faithful and True, and in righteousness he doth judge and make war.
> Revelation 19:11

King Jesus will bring an army for his second coming. There is no army at the rapture.

> And **the armies which were in heaven followed him upon white horses**, clothed in fine linen, white and clean. 15 And out of his mouth goeth a sharp sword, that with it he should smite the nations: and he shall rule them with a rod of iron: and he treadeth the winepress of the fierceness and wrath of Almighty God. 16 And he hath on his vesture and on his thigh a name written, KING OF KINGS, AND LORD OF LORDS.
> Revelation 19:14-16

When the church is raptured those left behind will go through the Tribulation. When Jesus returns the unsaved will be judged and thrown into the Lake of Fire.

> Then shall two be in the field; the one shall be taken, and the other left. 41 Two women shall be grinding at the mill; the one shall be taken, and the other left. 42 Watch therefore: for ye know not what hour your Lord doth come.
> Matthew 24:40-42

The main purpose of Jesus' second coming will be to defeat evil and restore the earth to its original intended glory. No longer will Satan roam this earth. The return of Jesus will be a terrifying time for those who refused him as their Savior. They will go through the battle of Armageddon (we will study this in more detail later) and the Great White Throne Judgement before they are cast into the lake of fire with Satan.

> And the devil that deceived them was cast into the lake of fire and brimstone, where the beast and the false prophet are, and shall be tormented day and night for ever and ever. 11 And I saw *a great white throne*, and him that sat on it, from whose face the earth and the heaven fled away; and there was found no place for them.12 And I saw the dead, small and great, stand before God; and the books were opened: and another book was opened, which is the book of life: and *the dead were judged* out of those things which were written in the books, according to their works. 13 And the sea gave up the dead which were in it: and death and hell delivered up the dead which were in them: and they were judged every man according to their works. 14 *And death and hell were cast into the lake of fire*. This is the second death. 15 And whosoever was not found written in the book of life was cast into the lake of fire.
>
> Revelation 20:10-15

When will Jesus' second coming take place? The Bible tells us immediately after the tribulation. He will gather the ones saved during the Tribulation to a safe place before the battle of Armageddon.

> ***Immediately after the tribulation*** of those days shall the sun be darkened, and the moon shall not give her light, and the stars shall fall from heaven, and the powers of the heavens shall be shaken: ³⁰ And then shall appear the sign of the Son of man in heaven: and then shall all the tribes of the earth mourn, and they shall see the Son of man coming in the clouds of heaven with power and great glory. ³¹ And he shall send his angels with a great sound of a trumpet, and they shall gather together his elect from the four winds, from one end of heaven to the other.
>
> Matthew 24:29-31

In conclusion, the rapture will take place when Jesus appears in the sky and calls those who accepted him as their Saviour home. The rapture takes place before the Tribulation. I believe this is when we receive our glorified bodies. The second coming of Jesus will take place at the end of the Tribulation when Jesus physically comes down on his white horse, battles evil, and executes his final judgement on the Antichrist, False Prophet, Satan, and the unsaved.

Beware I Will Come Again!

I came the first time in the name of love.
I came humbly as a child wrapped in swaddling clothes.
I suffered the things that men suffer.
I was tempted, tormented, and tortured.
I died and rose from the grave.
I covered your sins with my blood.
I showed you by example how to live.
I interceded before I died on your behalf,
   when to my Father I did plea:
   "Father, forgive them; for they know not what they do." (Luke 23:34)
I humbly died with a sign that said:
   "This Is Jesus The King Of The Jews." (Matthew 27:37)
I was buried and rose again,
So, you could have eternal life!

Beware I will come again and bring judgment.
I will come on a white horse fitting a King.
I bring with me war against evil.
My eyes will be like flames of fire,
And on my head will be many crowns.
My tongue will be a sharp sword,
I will press down upon you the wrath of Almighty God.
There shall be no doubt, as there was the first time, of whom I am.
   For on my thigh shall be written:
   "King of Kings, And Lord of Lords." (Revelation 19:16b)
Birds shall eat your flesh and,
   The Antichrist and False Prophet shall be thrown into the lake
of fire and brimstone.

Based on Revelation 19:11-21
--Deborah L. Gladwell—
   March 19, 2016

Heaven and End Times

1. John 14:1-3, What is the promise made?

2. John 14:3, Jesus said, "He will receive us unto **himself,** and we will be with him". Was he is talking about, the rapture of his church or his second coming?

3. 1 Thessalonians 4:16-17, Who will descend from Heaven and where does he stay?

4. 1 Thessalonians 4:16-17, Who will meet Jesus in the sky?

5. Matthew 24:40-42, This is a verse regarding the rapture. Will everyone on earth be raptured? Explain your answer.

6. Matthew 24:42, Do we know when Jesus will return to rapture us?

7. Matthew 24:43-44, Because we do not know when Jesus will rapture us, what should we be doing?

8. Matthew 24:29-31, When will Jesus' second coming take place?

9. Revelation 19:11, Who comes on a white horse and is this the rapture or Jesus' second coming?

10. Revelation 19:11, What will his purpose be?

11. Revelation 19:20, What will happen to the Antichrist and False Prophet?

12. Revelation 20:10, What happens to the devil?

13. Revelation 20:11-12, After Jesus returns, what Judgement will the unsaved experience?

14. Revelation 20:14, There will be no more death and those waiting in hell for judgement will be _____?

15. What is the main purpose of Jesus returning?

What is the Battle of Armageddon?

The Battle of Armageddon marks the end of the Tribulation period. During the period of Tribulation, many will not repent. They will take upon themselves the mark of the beast and practice evil doings. At this point, there will be no more chances of redemption for them. Although they endured perilous times, they will still be duked by Satan into thinking they can beat God.

What will happen to the people that accepted Jesus as their savior during the Tribulation? Will they be slaughtered by Jesus' army with the others? No, God's angels will gather them up. It does not appear that they are taken to Heaven but gathered into a place of safety.

> ***Immediately after the tribulation*** of those days shall the sun be darkened, and the moon shall not give her light, and the stars shall fall from heaven, and the powers of the heavens shall be shaken: *30* And then shall appear the sign of the Son of man in heaven: and then shall all the tribes of the earth mourn, and they shall see the ***Son of man coming in the clouds*** of heaven with power and great glory. *31* And he shall send ***his angels with a great sound of a trumpet, and they shall gather together his elect from the four winds, from one end of heaven to the other.***
>
> Matthew 24:29-31

> And I looked, and behold a white cloud, and upon the cloud one sat like unto the Son of man, having on his head a golden crown, and in his hand a sharp sickle *15* And another angel came out of the temple, crying with a loud voice to him that sat on the cloud, Thrust in thy sickle, and reap: for the time is come for thee to reap; for the harvest of the earth is ripe. *16* ***And he that sat on the cloud thrust in his sickle on the earth; and the earth was reaped.***
>
> Revelation 14:14-16

The Bible tells us that the Antichrist and the false prophet will send out miracle-working demons to the leaders of all countries to gather them to battle God. They will believe that with the whole world behind them they can defeat God.

> For they are the spirits of devils, working miracles, which go forth unto the kings of the earth and of the whole world, to gather them to the battle of that great day of God Almighty.
>
> Revelation 16:14

Jesus himself will lead the Battle of Armageddon. He will arrive on a white horse from Heaven, but he will not be alone!

> And I saw heaven opened, and behold a **white horse; and he that sat upon him was called Faithful and True**, and in righteousness he doth judge and make war...¹⁴And the **armies which were in heaven followed him** upon white horses, clothed in fine linen, white and clean. ¹⁵ And out of his mouth goeth a sharp sword, that with it he should smite the nations: and he shall rule them with a rod of iron: and **he treadeth the winepress** of the fierceness and wrath of Almighty God.
>
> Revelation 19:11,14-15

> And Enoch also, the seventh from Adam, prophesied of these, saying, Behold, the **Lord cometh with ten thousands of his saints**, ¹⁵ To execute judgment upon all, and to convince all that are ungodly among them of all their ungodly deeds which they have ungodly committed, and of all their hard speeches which ungodly sinners have spoken against him.
>
> Jude 1:14-15

The battle will be fought at Armageddon,

> And he gathered them together into a place called in the Hebrew tongue ***Armageddon.***
>
> Revelation 16:16

Scholars have conflicting opinions of where Armageddon is located. As I am not an expert, I will not try to figure out who is right. I just know it is a huge area. The Bible compares this last conflict to a winepress to illustrate the amount of blood that will be shed. Jesus will be the operator of this winepress.

> And the winepress was trodden without the city, **and blood came out of the winepress, even unto the horse bridles, by the space of a thousand and six hundred furlongs.**
>
> Revelation 14:20

> And out of his mouth goeth a sharp sword, that with it he should smite the nations: and he shall rule them with a rod of iron: **and he treadeth the winepress** of the fierceness and wrath of Almighty God.
>
> Revelation 19:15

This will be the bloodiest battle ever fought on earth. The Bible gives the measurements of the blood being "unto a horse bridles and 1600 furlongs." In our human minds, it is hard for us to fathom the vastness of a stream of blood that is about 4' deep and approximately 200 miles long. The width I do not know because we are not given it. All I can say is there will be way more blood than I ever want to see.

The Bible tells us that it will take seven months to bury the dead from this battle. and seven years to remove the weapons. Again, I cannot begin to fathom this.

> And they that dwell in the cities of Israel shall go forth, and shall set on fire and burn the weapons, both the shields and the bucklers, the bows and the arrows, and the handstaves, and the spears, and they shall burn them with fire seven years:
>
> Ezekiel 39:9

> And seven months shall the house of Israel be burying of them, that they may cleanse the land.
>
> Ezekiel 39:12

An interesting fact that I never really saw before is that the army that is with Jesus will not physically fight the enemies of Christ. *Jesus will defeat his enemies himself.* He will cast the Antichrist and False Prophet into the lake of fire burning with brimstone. He will slay those who followed them with his sword (words of his mouth). The birds will feast on their flesh, but they will not be tossed into the lake of fire until the Great White Throne Judgement.

> And I saw the beast, and the kings of the earth, and their armies, gathered together to make war against him that sat on the horse, and against his army. [20] *And the beast was taken, and with him the false prophet* that wrought miracles before him, with which he deceived them that had received the mark of the beast, and them that worshipped his image. ***These both were cast alive into a lake of fire burning with brimstone.*** [21] ***And the remnant were slain with the sword of him that sat upon the horse, which sword proceeded out of his mouth***: and ***all the <u>fowls</u> were filled with their flesh.***
>
> Revelation 19:19-21

> And, thou son of man, thus saith the Lord GOD; Speak unto every *feathered fowl*, and to every beast of the field, Assemble yourselves, and come; gather yourselves on every side to my sacrifice that I do sacrifice for you, even a great sacrifice upon the mountains of Israel, that *ye may eat flesh, and drink blood.*
>
> Ezekiel 39:17

Knowing Jesus as our Saviour is the only way of not having to go through this terrible time.

1. Matthew 24:29-31, and Revelation 14:14-16, At the end of the Tribulation what will happen to those that were saved during the Tribulation period?

2. Revelation 16:14, Why does the Antichrist and False Prophet send out miracle-working demons to the leaders of all countries?

3. Revelation 19:11, Who do you think is called Faithful and True?

4. Revelation 19:14, and Jude 1:14-15, Is Jesus alone? If not, who is with him?

5. Revelation 16:16, Where is this battle to be fought, and what is this battle called?

6. Revelation 19:15, The winepress represents bloodshed, who will be operating this winepress?

7. Revelation 14:20, How much blood will there be?

8. Ezekiel 39:9, How long will it take to burn and clean up the equipment left behind in this battle?

9. Ezekiel 39:12, How long will it take to bury the bodies?

10. Revelation 19:20, What happens to the Antichrist and False Prophet?

11. Revelation 19:21 and Ezekiel 39:17, What happens to the remnant of those that followed the Antichrist and False Prophet?

Millennial Reign of Christ?

Have you ever wondered why Satan will be contained for a thousand years or when the Millennial Reign will take place? Even more intriguing, what is the purpose of the Millennial Reign? All good questions.

Satan will not merely be placed in a cell for one thousand years. He will be chained and thrown into a bottomless pit. Then the pit will be sealed shut by God's angel.

> And I saw an angel come down from heaven, having the key of the bottomless pit and a great chain in his hand. 2 And he laid hold on the dragon, that old serpent, which is the Devil, and Satan, and bound him a thousand years, 3 And cast him into the bottomless pit, and shut him up, and set a seal upon him,
>
> Revelation 20:1-3a

This pit will not be a nice little stay at the Holiday Inn for Satan.

> And he opened the bottomless pit; and there arose a smoke out of the pit, as the smoke of a great furnace; and the sun and the air were darkened by reason of the smoke of the pit.
>
> Revelation 9:2

The smoke from the pit will pollute the air and darken the sun. It is a symbol of great evil and spiritual darkness.

During his thousand years of confinement, Satan will not be able to roam freely by air or ground. He will be void of all his evil powers and unable to influence humans to sin.

> that he should deceive the nations no more, till the thousand years should be fulfilled:
>
> Revelation 20:3b

The Millennial Reign of Christ will take place after the Tribulation and the Battle of Armageddon, but before the New Jerusalem (Heaven). The souls of martyred Christians (before and during the Tribulation), who were beheaded for their belief in Jesus and God, those who did not worship the Antichrist or his image, and those who did not take the mark of the beast, will reign with Jesus a thousand years.

> And I saw thrones, and they sat upon them, and judgment was given unto them: ***and I saw the souls of them that were beheaded for the witness of Jesus, and for the word of God, and which had not worshipped the beast, neither his image, neither had received his mark upon their foreheads, or in their hands; and they lived and reigned with Christ a thousand years.*** ⁵ But <u>*the rest of the dead lived not again until the thousand years were finished*</u>. This is the first resurrection. ⁶ ***Blessed and holy is he that hath part in the first resurrection***: on such the second death hath no power, but ***they shall be <u>priests of God and of Christ</u>, and shall reign with him a thousand years.***
>
> Revelation 20:4-6

Whoa, what about Christians that are not martyred? Although the above verses are confusing all Christians will be with Christ during his millennial rule. The first resurrection includes ***all*** who accepted Jesus as their Saviour. Christians will not be present at the second death. Verse five above is talking about the unsaved (rest of the dead), not Christians. The unsaved will not arise until the one thousand years are up, for judgement. Then they will be cast into the Lake of Fire. This is the second death.

God also tells John to write down some facts of things that will come. Please note verses seven and eight below.

> And he that sat upon the throne said, Behold, I make all things new. And he said unto me, ***Write: for these words are true and faithful.*** ⁶ And he said unto me, It is done. I am Alpha and Omega, the beginning and the end. I will give unto him that is athirst of the fountain of the water of life freely. ⁷ ***<u>He that overcometh shall inherit all things; and I will be his God, and he shall be my son.</u>*** ⁸ ***But the fearful, and unbelieving, and the abominable, and murderers, and whoremongers, and sorcerers, and idolaters, and all liars, shall have their part in the lake which burneth with fire and brimstone: which is the second death.***
>
> Revelation 21:5-8

We are joint-heirs with Christ. We are also kings and priests and promised to reign with him.

> And if children, then heirs; heirs of God, and joint-heirs with Christ; if so be that ***we suffer with him, that <u>we may be also glorified together</u>.***
>
> Romans 8:17
>
> If we suffer, <u>***we shall also reign with him***</u>: if we deny him, he also will deny us:
>
> 2 Timothy 2:12

> And hath *made us kings and priests unto God and his Father*; to him be glory and dominion for ever and ever. Amen.
>
> Revelation 1:6

> And hast *made us unto our God kings and priests*: and <u>we shall reign on the earth</u>.
>
> Revelation 5:10

The human population of the earth will consist of those who are alive and have accepted Jesus as their Saviour during the Tribulation. Remember Jesus reaped (gathered them) but they were not taken to Heaven. They will continue to live as humans and populate the earth. They will be taught the word of God and Jesus will live among them.

A more detailed description of the millennium is given in Isaiah. Some believe this is not the millennium but the new Jerusalem that is written about. This confusion stems from the words, "I create new heavens and a new earth:" But if you read on it does not say **new** Jerusalem.

> For, behold, I create new heavens and a new earth: and the former shall not be remembered, nor come into mind. ¹⁸ But be ye glad and rejoice for ever in that which I create: for, behold, I create *Jerusalem* a rejoicing, and her people a joy. ¹⁹ And I will rejoice in *Jerusalem*, and joy in my people: and the voice of weeping shall be no more heard in her, nor the voice of crying.
>
> Isaiah 65:17-19

God promises that in New Jerusalem there will be no more death.

> And God shall wipe away all tears from their eyes; and there shall be no more death, neither sorrow, nor crying, neither shall there be any more pain: for the former things are passed away.
>
> Revelation 21:4

Isaiah tells of death to those who do not accept Jesus before their one-hundredth birthday or who commit a crime of death at any age, therefore proving that this is the millennium.

> There shall be no more thence an infant of days, nor an old man that hath not filled his days: for the child shall die an hundred years old; but the sinner being an hundred years old shall be accursed.
>
> Isaiah 65:20

Man will dwell in homes they build and eat of the food they grow, and no one can steal from them.

> And they shall build houses, and inhabit them; and they shall plant vineyards, and eat the fruit of them. ²² They shall not build, and another inhabit; they shall not plant, and another eat: for as the days of a tree are the days of my people, and mine elect shall long enjoy the work of their hands. ²³ They shall not labour in vain, nor bring forth for trouble; for they are the seed of the blessed of the LORD, and their offspring with them.
> Isaiah 65:21-23

God will answer prayers before they are prayed.

> And it shall come to pass, that before they call, I will answer; and while they are yet speaking, I will hear.
> Isaiah 65:24

Man and animals will dwell peacefully together.

> The wolf and the lamb shall feed together, and the lion shall eat straw like the bullock: and dust shall be the serpent's meat. They shall not hurt nor destroy in all my holy mountain, saith the LORD.
> Isaiah 65:25

Then after a thousand years, something shocking happens, Satan will be turned loose.

> and after that he must be loosed a little season.
> Revelation 20:3c

Why in the world would God turn Satan loose again? The answer is for the final weeding process. In the next chapter, you will see Satan gathering up an army for the battle of Gog and Magog. These are the unsaved people still alive at the end of the millennium.

The millennium sounds good, but sin will still be present. Humans that live during this time cannot blame Satan for their unbelief and sins, because he was bound. You would think that with Jesus living among them no one would sin, but when Jesus came the first time man sinned.

Heaven and End Times

1. Revelation 20:1-3, In your own words, explain the meaning of these verses.

2. Revelation 9:2, Describe this pit?

3. What do you think the dark smoke that fills the air, symbolizes?

4. Revelation 20:4, Who does this verse say will reign with Jesus for a thousand years?

5. Revelation 20:5-6, Romans 8:17, 2 Timothy 2:12, Revelation 1:6, and Revelation 5:10, Will the saints that died before the Tribulation also rule with Jesus?

6. Revelation 20:5, Explain what the first resurrection means.

7. Revelation 20:6, What will those in the first resurrection become?

8. Revelation 20:6, What do you think the second death is?

9. Revelation 20:3, What will happen for a season?

10. Revelation 20:3, Why is Satan turned loose?

11. Isaiah 65:20, Will there be death during the thousand-year reign?

12. Isaiah 65:25, What will the living conditions of animals and humans be?

Battle of Gog and Magog and the Final Judgement

After the Millennial Reign of Christ, Satan will be turned loose. He will once again go to all the nations of the earth to gather an army to fight against Jesus and His followers.

> And when the thousand years are expired, Satan shall be loosed out of his prison, [8] And shall go out to deceive the nations which are in the four quarters of the earth, Gog, and Magog, to gather them together to battle: the number of whom is as the sand of the sea.
> Revelation 20:7-8

Gog and Magog are said to symbolize forces of evil that band together to fight God. The sad thing is that even though these people lived with Jesus, the number of those who reject Him will be as of the sand of the sea. That truly boggles my mind.

Satan and his army will encircle the saints and their beloved city. Some think this city is Jerusalem. But it matters not because God destroys them with fire.

> And they went up on the breadth of the earth, and compassed the camp of the saints about, and the beloved city: and fire came down from God out of heaven, and devoured them.
> Revelation 20:9

After the defeat of Satan and his army, Satan will be thrown into the Lake of Fire.

> And the devil that deceived them was cast into the lake of fire and brimstone, where the beast and the false prophet are, and shall be tormented day and night for ever and ever.
> Revelation 20:10

At the beginning of this book, we studied the Great White Throne Judgement. Well, this is when it takes place. The Antichrist, The False Prophet, and Satan have already been tossed into the Lake of Fire. God now raises all the dead people that never accepted Jesus as their saviour. The first set of books are the records of every unsaved person's life's deeds, which they will be judged according to their works (good or bad). The book of life will also be there, but I believe that it is there to show them that their names are not in this book. They will quiver because they had every opportunity to accept Jesus and have their name in this book. They are not ignorant of what the book of life is. Each at some point in their life was told the plan of salvation and willfully rejected it.

> And I saw a great white throne, and him that sat on it, from whose face the earth and the heaven fled away; and there was found no place for them. [12] And I saw the dead, small and great, stand before God; and the books were opened: and another book was opened, which is the book of life: and the dead were judged out of those things which were written in the books, according to their works. [13] And the sea gave up the dead which were in it; and death and hell delivered up the dead which were in them: and they were judged every man according to their works.
> Revelation 20:11-13

We are told death and hell will be thrown into the Lake of Fire. This means that there will be no more physical death for those who accepted Jesus as their savior. Since there will be no more sin or physical death there will be no need for a holding place (hell) for unsaved people to be held. Everyone whose name is not found in the book of life will be thrown into the Lake of Fire. This is called the second death because these people will be forever separated from God.

> And death and hell were cast into the lake of fire. This is the second death. [15] And whosoever was not found written in the book of life was cast into the lake of fire.
> Revelation 20:14-15

The good news is all things will be new. God will now live amongst us. We will be his people and He will be our God. There will be no more tears, death, sorrow, crying, or pain.

> And I saw a new heaven and a new earth: for the first heaven and the first earth were passed away; and there was no more sea. [2] And I John saw the holy city, new Jerusalem, coming down from God out of heaven, prepared as a bride adorned for her husband. [3] And I heard a great voice out of heaven saying, Behold, the tabernacle of God is with men, and he will dwell with them, and they shall be his people, and God himself shall be with them, and be their God. [4] And

God shall wipe away all tears from their eyes; and there shall be no more death, neither sorrow, nor crying, neither shall there be any more pain: for the former things are passed away.
⁵And he that sat upon the throne said, Behold, I make all things new. And he said unto me, Write: for these words are true and faithful.

Revelation 21:1-5

Heaven and End Times

1. Revelation 20:7, What will happen at the end of the 1,000-year reign?

2. Revelation 20:8, We are told that Satan will deceive the nations. Does this sound a lot like another famous story of deception in the Bible? If yes, who was deceived by Satan at the beginning of time?

3. Revelation 20:8, Why was Satan gathering these people?

4. Revelation 20:8, Who or what is Gog and Magog?

5. Revelation 20:9, Satan and his army surround Jesus and the saints. What happens to them?

6. Revelation 20:10, What will immediately happen to Satan?

7. Revelation 20:11-13, What takes place at this time?

8. Revelation 20:14, What is thrown into the Lake of Fire? Explain what this means.

9. Revelation 20:14-15, Explain in your own words what, "this is the second death", means.

10. Revelation 21:1, What will happen?

11. Revelation 21:2, What did John see?

12. Revelation 21:3, The tabernacle of God will be with men. Who will live with man and what will we be to God?

13. Revelation 21:3, What will God be to us?

14. Revelation 21:4, What are the five things that will be no more?

15. Revelation 21:5, What will God make all things?

Alpha and Omega!

After God showed John what was going to take place in the End Times, He point-blank told John who he is (the Alpha and Omega). He also told him to write down what he said.

> And he that sat upon the throne said, Behold, I make all things new. And he said unto me, ***Write: for these words are true and faithful***. ⁶And he said unto me, It is done. ***I am Alpha and Omega, the beginning and the end***. I will give unto him that is athirst of the fountain of the water of life freely. ⁷***He that overcometh shall inherit all things; and I will be his God, and he shall be my son.*** ⁸***But the fearful, and unbelieving, and the abominable, and murderers, and whoremongers, and sorcerers, and idolaters, and all liars, shall have their part in the lake which burneth with fire and brimstone: which is the second death.***
>
> Revelation 21:5-8

In our small minds, we find it confusing how someone can have no beginning or end. For many years I have heard it explained this way; draw a complete circle or infinity symbol. If drawn correctly you cannot tell where it began or where it ends. The same philosophy applies to God. He was there before creation, he is infinite. He will be there for us in the New Jerusalem (Heaven on earth) and forever.

The Holy Trinity (The Father, The Son, and The Holy Ghost) also confuse us. We cannot fathom that they are three separate beings in one. God is the creator, Jesus is part God and part man, who died for our sins and rose again. Jesus is our Saviour. The Holy Spirit (God's spirit) was sent to us after Jesus departed to draw us to God, to help us understand God's word, to convict us unto salvation, and to comfort us. Some also refer to the Holy Trinity as the Godhead. I mention all this to explain why some verses reference the name Jesus and some reference God. They are separate but the same.

We know that the term and meaning of Alpha and Omega are very important or they would not be mentioned so many times in the Bible.

OLD TESTAMENT
- Isaiah 44:6 Thus saith the Lord the King of Israel, and his redeemer the **Lord of hosts**; *I am the first, and I am the last*; and **beside me there is no God.**
- Isaiah 48:12 Hearken unto me, O Jacob and Israel, my called; *I am he; I am the first, I also am the last.*

NEW TESTAMENT

- (God) John 1:1 In the beginning was the **Word**, and the Word was with God, and the Word was **God**.
  - If you notice Word is capitalized as God always is in the Bible. I point this out to prove God was here in the beginning.
- (Jesus) Revelation 19:13 And he was clothed with a vesture dipped in blood: and his name is called The Word of God.
  - When Jesus returns for the battle of Armageddon, he will be wearing a vesture (robe) and he is called, "The Word of God."
- (God) Revelation 21:6-7 And he said unto me, It is done. I am Alpha and Omega, the beginning and the end. I will give unto him that is athirst of the fountain of the water of life freely. 7 He that overcometh shall inherit all things; and I will be his God, and he shall be my son.
  - God declares the end
- (God) Revelation 21:3 And I heard a great voice out of heaven saying, Behold, the tabernacle of God is with men, and he will dwell with them, and they shall be his people, and God himself shall be with them, and be their God.
  - God shall live with us
- (Jesus) Revelation 22:12-13 And, behold, I come quickly; and my reward is with me, to give every man according as his work shall be. 13 I am Alpha and Omega, the beginning and the end, the first and the last.
  - Jesus will be over the final Judgement

When we think about the Alpha and the Omega we should be in awe of God and give Him the honor, glory, praise, and respect as such. Below you see the word fear. In the Bible that often means respect not afraid.

> *By the word of the Lord were the heavens made; and all the host of them by the breath of his mouth.* 7 He gathereth the waters of the sea together as an heap: he layeth up the depth in storehouses. 8 Let all the earth fear the Lord: let all the inhabitants of the world stand in awe of him. 9 *For he spake, and it was done; he commanded, and it stood fast.*
>
> Psalm 33:6-9

In conclusion, even though it baffles our minds the Bible teaches that God is truly the Alpha and Omega. The Bible is the word of God which we are not to add or subtract from.

> What thing soever I command you, observe to do it: thou shalt not add thereto, nor diminish from it.
>
> Deuteronomy 12:32

Jesus Is!

He is the Alpha and Omega.
He was here in the beginning and
He will be here in the end.

He is the only way to Heaven,
The Savior of men.

He is the Good Shepherd,
Taking care of his flock.

Because of our sins, he was crucified.
He died and was buried,
But thank God from the tomb he did arise!

-Deborah L. Gladwell-

Heaven and End Times

1. Revelation 21:5, God tells John to write what he says and that the words he writes are _____ & _____.

2. Concerning the above answers, why do you think God said these words?

3. Revelation 21:5, Do you feel that God wants John to inform people of what will happen if they continue to live in sin?

4. Revelation 21:6, God says he is the Alpha and the Omega. What does he say that this means?

5. Revelation 21:7, God told John that those who overcome evil shall inherit Heaven and He will be our God and we will be his _____?

6. Revelation 21:8, What will happen to those who do not respect God, to the unsaved, and to those who commit all types of abominations?

7. Psalm 33:8, We should be in _____ of God?

8. Psalm 33:9, Why should we respect and be in awe of God?

9. Deuteronomy 12:32, Proverbs 30:5-6, and Revelation 22:18-19, The Bible clearly says that God is the Alpha and the Omega. Just because we do not understand, should we say it is not true, and it means something different than the beginning and the end? Explain..

What is a World Without Hope?

In 2019 into the 20s our world began to run wild in fear of a deadly virus called Covid19. Some people lost all forms of human kindness and decency. Others mentally broke down and became hoarders of toilet paper. Some were spitefully hoping that **we the people** go bankrupt just to get even with a man they did not like (President Donald Trump).

Our President said he was hopeful a certain medicine might work, and for that, he was ridiculed for giving false hope. Since when is it bad to have and give hope? Did we not fight the Revolutionary War with the **hope** of freedom?

God gave us hope from the beginning of time. You can take any promise of God to the bank because it will be fulfilled.

> Paul, a servant of God, and an apostle of Jesus Christ, according to the faith of ***God's elect***, and the acknowledging of the truth which is after godliness; [2] ***In hope of eternal life, which God, that cannot lie, promised before the world began***; [3] But hath in due times manifested his word through preaching, which is committed unto me according to the commandment of God our Saviour;
>
> Titus 1:1-3

WHAT IS HOPE AND WHAT DOES HOPE DO FOR MANKIND?

We cannot see our faith so we must hope in what we cannot see. We are told that we are to have the patience to see the fulfillment of our hope.

> Now ***faith is the substance of things hoped for***, the ***evidence of things not seen.***
>
> Hebrews 11:1

> But if ***we hope for that we see not***, then do we ***with patience wait for it***.
>
> Romans 8:25

Hope makes us strong,

> But they that wait upon ***the Lord shall renew their strength***; they shall mount up with wings as eagles; they shall run, and not be weary; and they shall walk, and not faint.
>
> Isaiah 40:31

Hope fills us with joy and peace,

> Now the **God of hope fill you with all joy and peace** in believing, that ye may abound in hope, through the power of the Holy Ghost.
> Romans 15:13

Hope makes us unashamed,

> *And hope maketh not ashamed*; because the love of God is shed abroad in our hearts by the Holy Ghost which is given unto us.
> Romans 5:5

The Bible warns us there will come a day that we will have to explain our faith and yes, our hope. Is that day now? Think about it, bars were opened before churches.

> But sanctify the Lord God in your hearts: and be ready always to ***give an answer to every man that asketh you a reason of the hope that is in you*** with meekness and fear:
> 1 Peter 3:15

Do not let anyone or any situation take away your hope because God is our hope. He is our hope in both good and bad times. He will be our only hope to cling to as we approach End Times. Always keep your eyes on God, not man. Man will fail you, but God will not.

Proverbs exactly sum up a world without hope. It says that if you have no hope, your heart will be sick. But when you have hope it is like a tree of life.

> ***Hope deferred maketh the heart sick***: but when the desire cometh, it is a tree of life.
> Proverbs 13:12

I conclude that a world without hope is a lost world! When all hope has vanished we are more than likely in or very close to the End Times.

1. Titus 1:2-3, God promised eternal life to His elect (those saved) from the beginning of time. How do we know this will happen?

2. Jeremiah 29:11, God thinks of each of us individually. His thoughts are of _____ not _____?

3. Hebrews 11:1, Tells us that faith is for things hoped for. What do you think this means?

4. Romans 8:25, Tells us if we are hoping for what we cannot see, we must be what?

5. Isaiah 40:31, What does this verse say hope will make us?

6. Romans 15:13, What does the God of hope fill us with?

7. Romans 5:5, Hope makes us what?

8. 1 Peter 3:15, If an unsaved person should ask you about your hope, what must you be ready to do?

9. 1 Peter 1:3, What kind of hope does God give us by the resurrection of Jesus Christ?

10. Proverbs 13:12, If you have no hope, it will make you _____?

11. Describe in your own words, what the world would be like with no hope.

What the Bible Says About the Importance of History

The Bible tells us before End Times there will be a falling away. People will love themselves, have no natural affection for life, they will be false accusers, and diseases will increase. We have witnessed many of these things in our society.

From 2018 to the early '20s many sought to destroy history by tearing down altars, churches, monuments, and statues, rewriting history books, or just plain deleting the history they do not like. Are we in the falling away state that the Bible talks about? Only God knows.

The Bible is the number one selling book every single year, why? Because not only is the Bible an instruction book divinely written for God's children, but the Bible itself is a history book. It contains all things from the past and the things of the future, which guide our present.

The Bible includes documented history of all the mistakes God's people made in the past which includes wars, peace, famine, foreign policy, genealogy, sexual behavior, etc. There is nothing new, as far as human behavior today, that has not taken place in the past. In other words, HISTORY!

> The thing that hath been, it is that which shall be; and that which is done is that which shall be done: and ***there is no new thing under the sun.*** 10 Is there any thing whereof it may be said, See, this is new? ***it hath been already of old time, which was before us.***
> Ecclesiastes 1:9-10

The importance of History is to learn from past mistakes and not repeat them. God, through the Bible, tells us to heed the lessons of history,

> ***For whatsoever things were written aforetime were written for our learning***, that we through patience and comfort of the scriptures might have hope.
> Romans 15:4

> ***Now all these things happened unto them for examples: and they are written for our admonition***, upon whom the ends of the world are come.
> 1 Corinthians 10:11

Surprise, altars, monuments, and statues are nothing new to any society. Let us look at their purpose.

ALTARS

- The Bible teaches that throughout history, after something major happened an Altar was built. Why? To be a remembrance to man of what happened at a particular place and time in history. An altar also commemorated an encounter with God.
    - Exodus 20:24 An altar of earth thou shalt make unto me, and shalt sacrifice thereon thy burnt offerings, and thy peace offerings, thy sheep, and thine oxen: in all places where I record my name I will come unto thee, and I will bless thee
- The first *Altar* in the Bible was built by Noah after the Great Flood.
    - Genesis 8:20a And Noah builded an altar unto the LORD;"
        - This altar, along with many others named in the Bible, was pre-Jesus, and most included sacrifice. Later, Jesus became our ultimate(final) sacrifice, therefore, after his death, burial, and resurrection those who called upon his name needed no physical sacrifice at the altar, which is now found in two places. A physical altar in a church or a spiritual altar in our heart.

MONUMENTS

Teaching tools: to provide answers for future generations. The Bible tells us of two such monuments in Joshua.

- Joshua 4:4-7 Then Joshua called the twelve men, whom he had prepared of the children of Israel, out of every tribe a man: [5] And Joshua said unto them, Pass over before the ark of the LORD your God into the midst of Jordan, and take you up every man of you a stone upon his shoulder, according unto the number of the tribes of the children of Israel: [6] ***That this may be a sign among you, that when your children ask their fathers in time to come, saying, What mean ye by these stones?*** [7] Then ye shall answer them, That the waters of Jordan were cut off before the ark of the covenant of the LORD; when it passed over Jordan, the waters of Jordan were cut off: and these stones shall be for a *memorial* unto the children of Israel for ever.
    - (This monument was built in Gilgal. See Joshua 4:20)
- Joshua 4:9-10 And Joshua set up twelve stones in the midst of Jordan, in the place where the feet of the priests which bare the ark of the

covenant stood: and they are there unto this day. 10 For the priests which bare the ark stood in the midst of Jordan, until everything was finished that the Lord commanded Joshua to speak unto the people, according to all that Moses commanded Joshua: and the people hasted and passed over.
- o This monument was built in the middle of the Jordan to commemorate where the priest stood when God parted the river

Contracts with God: (not a complete list of monuments for contracts)
- Joshua set up a monument to commemorate the contract made between Israel and God that they would not worship idols.
  - o Joshua 24:26-27 And Joshua wrote these words in the book of the law of God, and took a ***great stone***, and set it up there under an oak, that was by the sanctuary of the LORD. 27 And Joshua said unto all the people, Behold, this stone shall be a witness unto us; for it hath heard all the words of the LORD which he spake unto us: it shall be therefore a witness unto you, lest ye deny your God.
- God changed Jacob's name to Israel and made a covenant with him and Jacob created a monument.
  - o Genesis 35:12-15 And the land which I gave Abraham and Isaac, to thee I will give it, and to thy seed after thee will I give the land. 13 And God went up from him in the place where he talked with him. 14 And Jacob set up a pillar in the place where he talked with him, even a pillar of stone: and he poured a drink offering thereon, and he poured oil thereon. 15 And Jacob called the name of the place where God spake with him, Bethel.

Deliverance:
- God rescued the Israelites from the Philistines.
  - o 1 Samuel 7:12 Then Samuel took a stone, and set it between Mizpeh and Shen, and called the name of it Ebenezer, saying, Hitherto hath the LORD helped us.

Important People: (Good and bad) Absalom was not a good person, but he built a pillar to commemorate his burial place.
- 2 Samuel 18:18 Now Absalom in his lifetime had taken and reared up for himself a pillar, which is in the king's dale: for he said, I have no son to keep my name in remembrance: and he called the pillar after his own name: and it is called unto this day, Absalom's place.

Promise:
- Isaiah 19:19-20 In that day shall there be an altar to the LORD in the midst of the land of Egypt, and a pillar at the border thereof to the LORD. [20] And it shall be for a sign and for a witness unto the LORD of hosts in the land of Egypt: *for they shall cry unto the LORD because of the oppressors, and he shall send them a saviour, and a great one, and he shall deliver them.*

STATUES

Idolatry: Later, you will see God lets statues be built, but not for idolatry purposes.
- God warns about idol worshipping of angels in heaven or Satan, fallen angels or demons in Hell.
    - Exodus 20:4-5a Thou shalt not make unto thee any graven image, or any likeness of any thing that is in heaven above, or that is in the earth beneath, or that is in the water under the earth. [5] Thou shalt not bow down thyself to them, nor serve them: for I the LORD thy God am a jealous God,
- God warned that he never showed us his form, so we were not to make any image of Him, because we do not know his image.
    - Deuteronomy 4:15-16a Take ye therefore good heed unto yourselves; for ye saw no manner of similitude on the day that the LORD spake unto you in Horeb out of the midst of the fire: [16] Lest ye corrupt yourselves, and make you a graven image, the similitude of any figure,
- After the birth of Jesus, man visually saw a physical form of the likeness of God. Many scholars believe that because of this it is now okay to make statues of Jesus.
    - John 1:14 And the Word was made flesh, and dwelt among us, (and we beheld his glory, the glory as of the only begotten of the Father,) full of grace and truth.

Lesson: Although God warned us of worshiping statues(idols), He also had statues built to teach lessons to wayward people. Statues should be used for the same purpose today, to teach right and wrong. To remind us of the good and to warn us of repeating the bad. Statues show us what we have overcome and accomplished throughout history.
- Snakes were biting the Israelites and causing great burning pain. The

people complained to Moses and God had him make a statue. This statue was a lesson of faith.
- o Numbers 21:8-9 And the LORD said unto Moses, ***Make thee a fiery serpent, and set it upon a pole***: and it shall come to pass, that every one that is bitten, when he looketh upon it, shall live. ⁹ And Moses made a serpent of brass, and put it upon a pole, and it came to pass, that if a serpent had bitten any man, when he beheld the serpent of brass, he lived.
- God had two cherubims made for the Ark of the Covenant. These angels were not made to worship but as a symbol of Angels protecting the Ark of God as they did the entrance to the Garden of Eden.
  - o Exodus 25:18 And thou shalt make two cherubims of gold, of beaten work shalt thou make them, in the two ends of the mercy seat.

In conclusion, the Bible is the best history book in the world. It is packed full of information going back to the creation of our world. It is not full of perfect people but of imperfect people. If we were all perfect no one would need God, we could do everything ourselves. Even David who was loved by God was VERY flawed. Just because someone said, thought, or did something in their past, does not mean past errors should cancel out all the good they did in their life. So, before you start burning and tearing down Altars, Monuments and Statues, think of the good they do, what lessons could be learned (good or bad), and most importantly do not repeat the bad.

I leave you with this question, why do you think Satan wants history erased? Could it be that it would make his job a whole lot easier as we approach end times?

Deborah L. Gladwell

1. Ecclesiastes 1:9-10, Is there any new crime or sin in today's world?

2. Romans 15:4, The Bible is a history book. Why does it say history was recorded?

3. 1 Corinthians 10:11, Why do things happen throughout history?

4. Exodus 20:24, Why were altars built in the Bible?

5. Genesis 8:20a, This was the _____ altar recorded in the Bible?

6. Joshua 4:4-10, This monument was used as a _____ tool for future generations?

7. Joshua 24:26-27, and Genesis 35:12-15, What was the purpose of these monuments?

8. 1 Samuel 7:12, What was the significance of this monument?

9. 2 Samuel 18:18, What was the purpose of this monument?

10. Isaiah 19:19-20, This monument was what to the people?

11. Exodus 20:4-5a, What did God say not to build and why?

12. Exodus 20:4-5a, Are we to worship angels, Satan, fallen angels, etc.?

13. Deuteronomy 4:15-16a, We are not to build statues of God, why?

14. John 1:14, Who has man seen?

15. Do you think it is okay to make statues of Jesus? This clearly is an opinion matter.

16. Numbers 21:8-9, What lesson can we learn here?

17. Exodus 25:18, Were these Angels made to worship?

18. Do you think that history is an important tool to keep people from making the same mistakes that have already been made in the past?